Literature Circles

• • • • • • • • •

Contents

· · · · · · · · ·

Acknowledgments

Like my six previous books, this one owes its largest thanks to the teachers I'm privileged to call colleagues and friends. In my roles as a teacher educator, writing project co-director, and researcher, I spend a lot of time in other people's classrooms, borrowing ideas. From Chicago's inner city to its cosmopolitan suburbs to the rural schools downstate, scores of generous teachers have lent me their students, their time, and their space to try out and observe ideas about literature and learning. Many of these professionals' best ideas appear in their own words in Chapters 6 and 7, and their other wisdoms and insights are stranded through every page of this volume. To all of these treasured colleagues, my deepest thanks.

This idea-stealing habit has also put me in touch with some wonderful school districts and great school leaders. No partners have been more significant to my own growth than the teachers and administrators of Orland Park, Illinois, and especially its Assistant Superintendent for Curriculum, Jean Smith. I don't know another public school person who combines Jean's synoptic knowledge of curriculum with her steady and savvy approach to change. For nearly ten years, in this diverse and fast-growing district, we've worked at broad-based teacher-led renewal, first in reading and language arts, and more recently across the curriculum, as we've tried to devise progressive and authentic assessments for all subjects and grades. Nor will I soon forget Superintendent Tom Pauley's well-timed and riveting speeches to our curriculum committees. "Are you doing what's right for the kids?" he'd ask when we got nervous about the political implications of the changes we were designing. "Then let me worry about the test scores and the phone calls," he'd say, taking a donut back to his office and leaving us to innovate without fear or limits.

Baker Demonstration School has long been close to my heart, since its teachers are my university colleagues and because my own children have been so well educated there. In a total of fourteen kid-years at Baker (so far), Nick and Marny have enjoyed the most consistently creative and dedicated group of educators I've ever known. For many years, I couldn't quite put my finger on what common feature held the Dem School's magnificent but diverse faculty together, but recently I figured it out. Above all, Baker teachers invite and prize children's *expression,* in every possible medium—art, talk, writing, drama, dance, hypercard stacks, publishing, storytelling. This nurturing of expression has carried over to our home, where Marny's pictures, sculptures, and art supplies take up every square inch not already occupied by galleys of Nick's B-movie fanzine and its attendant international correspondence.

The whole family of Washington Irving School in Chicago, including the parents, kids, teachers, and principal Madeleine Maraldi, have offered me a warming and growthful friendship over the last five years. Every day of the school year, Irving contradicts the negative myths propounded about inner-city schools, minority students, and urban teachers. Highlights of our collaboration have included countless after-school workshops, "family album night," starring in a PBS documentary, and the summer of 1994, when twenty-two of us went on retreat together to the woods of northern Michigan. Now we're planning our own high school, so that the kids graduating from Irving and schools like it will have a progressive, democratic, holistic alternative for their teenage years.

My Cajun compatriots from the Lafayette, Louisiana Parish Schools have spiced up my understanding of whole language throughout our three years of work together, both down in their bayous and up in my own pine woods. Carolyn Levy, the queen of the Cajuns, not only shared her secret recipe for crayfish étoufée, she also showed me how a change agent can be principled, steadfast, and persistent—while also remaining good-humored and gracious.

I have been delighted to work with Barbara Unikel in two locations, first when she was principal of South School in Glencoe, Illinois and more recently in Northbrook School District 27, where she serves as Assistant Superintendent for Instruction. Barbara's innovative program of districtwide professional development is based upon teacher choice and teacher leadership, and could serve as a model for schools around the country. Carol Haynes,

Coordinator for Reading and Language Arts in Hinsdale District 181, has given me a chance to work over several years with a variety of K–8 teachers who have contributed much to my understanding of reading and writing.

When I heard that Philippa Stratton and Tom Seavey were starting Stenhouse Publishers, I decided immediately that I wanted this book to be on their first list. Through their years at Heinemann Educational Books, Philippa and Tom placed before American teachers a series of books that has changed the quality of classroom life for hundreds of thousands of students across the country. Not only are Philippa and Tom wise editors and skillful book-birthers, they are also a delight to work with. Just as I expected, preparing this first Stenhouse volume has been a pleasant adventure, filled with laughs, faxes, surprises, disks, drafts, plot twists, computer glitches, occasional melodrama, and several jolly dinners in assorted American cities. It has been, as we say in Chicago, a slice.

My colleagues at National Louis-University's Center for City Schools—Marilyn Bizar, Barbara Morris, Patricia Bearden, and Art Hyde— are a constant source of support, inspiration, and amusement—often simultaneously. Steve Zemelman, with whom I've written three other books, has undoubtedly enjoyed this respite from collaboration with me, but he nevertheless chipped in his usual assortment of valuable ideas and constructive challenges. The miraculous Flynns, Sharon and Jeff, who co-direct the Walloon Institute with me, make it possible for us to have a magical summer retreat where teachers from all over the world gather to share ideas about literature circles and other student-centered practices. But as always, my greatest personal support comes from Elaine Daniels—my beloved partner, friend, and fellow teacher. Thanks again.

• • • • • • • • •

Contributing Teachers

Judith Alford
Maplewood School
Cary, IL

Bonnie Barelli
Tioga School
Bensenville, IL

Barbara Dress
Illinois Writing Project
Palatine, IL

Judith Epcke
Shabonee School
Northbrook, IL

Marianne Flanagan
Metcalfe Magnet School
Chicago, IL

Cheryl Foertsch
Centennial School
Orland Park, IL

Ruth Freedman
Baker Demonstration
School
Evanston, IL

Linda Fulton
Orland Center School
Orland Park, IL

Pat Gardner
Centennial School
Orland Park, IL

Debbie Gurvitz
Lyon School
Glenview, IL

Judith Hechler
South School
Des Plaines, IL

Sandy King
Marion Jordan School
Palatine, IL

Marianne Kroll
Palos East School
Palos Heights, IL

Debra O'Connor
Centennial School
Orland Park, IL

Jayne O'Neill
Centennial School
Orland Park, IL

Ann Paziotopoulos
Palos East School
Palos Heights, IL

Marline Pearson
Madison Area Technical
College
Madison, WI

Suzy Ruder
Carl Sandburg High
School
Orland Park, IL

Sally Ryan
Baker Demonstration
School
Evanston, IL

Becky Abraham Searle
Whiteley School
Hoffman Estates, IL

Donna-Marie Stupple
Maine East High School
Park Ridge, IL

Maria Ward
Glenbard East High
School
Lombard, IL

Sharon Weiner
Baker Demonstration
School
Evanston, IL

• • • • • • • •

Beginnings

This structure allowed me the freedom to turn ownership over to the students. Students gained greater insight by sharing literature instead of reading in isolation. Students who never participated before during whole-class discussion found a voice.
—Sandy Niemiera, fourth-grade teacher

Karen Smith

It is the summer of 1982, and Karen Smith is preparing for another year of teaching fifth grade at Lowell School in Phoenix, Arizona. Claire Staab, a friend and teaching colleague who is moving to British Columbia, comes by to offer Karen some classroom leftovers. Among the castoff items is a box of assorted paperback novels—three copies of this title, four or five of that, six of another. Because she can always use extra books for independent reading in her class, Karen cheerfully accepts her friend's donation. She sticks the box of books in the back of the room, and then, amid the excitement and turmoil of starting a new year, forgets about them.

A couple of months later, a group of students discovers the box. Sifting through the books, the kids get excited and approach Ms. Smith for permission to read them. Assuming the kids are simply prowling for more independent reading titles, Karen casually gives her approval. But within a few days, she notices that the students have chosen books, established groups around their choices, assigned themselves pages to read, and are meeting regularly to talk about their books. She sits in on a couple of the groups and is dazzled by the quality, depth, range, and energy of the talk she hears. Karen's ten-year-old students have just invented their own literature circles.

Because Karen Smith was an extraordinary teacher (that very fall, she had been reading about Louise Rosenblatt's reader response literary theory and Daniel Fader's "hooked on books" program), she immediately recognized the significance of the kids' invention. They had created a structure that allowed powerful, student-initiated, high-order discussion and thinking to go on around good books. Karen quickly moved to make these emergent discussion circles official—not to tame their spontaneity but to make sure that all kids in the class got involved.

In 1982, Karen was also a graduate student at Arizona State University, so she invited colleagues and professors into her classroom to observe the kids' groups at work and help her puzzle out the next steps. First among these was Ralph Peterson, who helped Karen figure out how to join the kids' book-talks without dominating the interaction. Soon, other leaders of the profession, including Dorothy Watson and Jerome Harste, came to visit, were impressed by the students, offered their insights on the process, and began to spread the word around the country of the wonderful structure invented by Karen Smith's fifth graders. A few years later, Karen herself told the story of these literature groups and the rest of her reading program in *Talking About Books* (Short and Mitchell Pierce 1990).

Marianne Flanagan

It is the fall of 1993, on the south side of Chicago. After a budget crisis that delayed the start of school by a week, Marianne Flanagan's fifth graders have finally come back to school. Now, just a few days into the year, these thirty-two black and Hispanic students are already fully engaged in their literature circles. These discussion groups have many similarities with the ones invented by Karen Smith's kids a decade ago and a half-continent away. . . .

You hear the noise long before you reach the door to room 213 in Metcalfe School: the buzz of literature circles echoes halfway down the stairwell. When you first enter the room, you may not believe that any reliable communication can happen amid the din in this too-small room; indeed, that's exactly what Marianne's colleagues, long bred to equate silence with effective teaching, seem to think as they walk past her doorway, shaking their heads. And yet as you get acclimated to the noise level, join a few student groups, and tune in to the ongoing conversations, the sophisticated quality of these literary discussions becomes apparent.

Children are tucked up close to each other, ten-year-olds talking with animation, seriousness, and sometimes passion about the novels they have chosen to read. They have come to class with notes and drawings reflecting their ideas about the day's reading. They toss searching and open-ended questions into their groups, read aloud favorite passages, stop to talk about difficult or powerful words. They are constantly flipping back through their books, using specific passages to prove points or settle disagreements. They laugh a lot, argue some, often touch each other to stress a point, and keep one eye on the clock to make sure everyone gets their fair share of "airtime."

Among the titles being discussed today are Katherine Paterson's *Bridge to Terabithia*, H. G. Wells's *War of the Worlds*, Beverly Cleary's *Dear Mr. Henshaw*, and Sid Fleischmann's *The Whipping Boy*. Because Marianne's class is just beginning with literature circles, they are using a set of simple, rotating roles that are one of the chief innovations to be described in this book. These different roles help students to surface and independently discuss important topics of their own, rather than march through typical teacher-supplied study questions. Among the roles Marianne's kids are using today are discussion director, literary luminary, connector, illustrator, and vocabulary enricher.

Over in the corner, Brian, Wilbert, and Roy are completely engrossed in their discussion of Elizabeth Speare's *Sign of the Beaver*. The colonial family in the story has been forced to move to the remote Penobscot region because the parents could not find work in the city of Boston. Wilbert, acting as today's "connector," shares a personal experience: "My Dad lost his job. We're not poor like the kid in the book, but he did lose his job." The kids talk quietly for a few minutes about family economic problems. Roy, who is today's discussion director, wonders aloud whether a twelve-year-old boy should be left alone like this, in the woods for six weeks with only a rifle and some food. The boys enter a lively debate, centering around the possibility of Indian attacks. Roy doesn't think the one-shot, muzzle-loading gun would be much help: "Man, they'd send lots of Indians with lots of arrows," he says. "They'd shoot you before you could get them." Wilbert suggests that maybe if Matt got really good with the gun, he might "grow up to be a cop or something." Roy laughs and Brian chimes in: "Not in 1768! This isn't *now*, you know." They all have good laugh at Wilbert's anachronism.

Again the conversation returns to Indian attacks. Roy argues that because Matt has already met and talked to one member of the local tribe, such attacks are unlikely. "If you make friends with one Indian, then you're friends with them all," he asserts positively. Brian and Wilbert insist that Matt is still in danger. Suddenly, Roy's face lights up. "It's like what's-her-name," he says. "You know—that girl. . . ." And with that, he springs out of his chair and starts poking around in people's desks, looking for something. He rummages through half the room before he finds what he's looking for. Meanwhile, Brian and Wilbert just shake their heads and continue talking about whether or not their fathers would let them have a gun. Finally, Roy returns to the circle in triumph, carrying a thick U.S. history textbook. Flipping through the pages, he slaps the book down, open to an illustration of Captain John Smith and Pocahontas. "See," Roy announces, "if you were friends with one Indian, you were friends with them all!"

Marianne skirts around the edges, dipping briefly into the groups. Often, she gets drawn into the conversation if the book is one she has read herself—indeed, Marianne enjoys the books so much that she often gets stuck in one group when she had planned to circulate through several. She hasn't even preread every book kids are discussing, but she doesn't worry about whether she is "really teaching." There are other scheduled times during the school day when Marianne is very much in charge of the material and the process, selecting readings, offering interpretations, modeling strategies, and drawing kids' attention to an author's craft. Perhaps if she were conducting a teacher-directed lesson on *Sign of the Beaver,* Marianne might have gently challenged Roy's still-stereotypic thinking about Indians and their friendships. But this is not the time.

This chunk of the day—literature circle time—is separate and different and special. This is time for kids to pick, read, and discuss their own books. Marianne is happy to see the kids connecting with books, taking responsibility as readers and group members, constructing meaning together, and beginning to debate and challenge one another. She knows that in running literature circles, the teacher's main job is not to translate or interpret the books, but to facilitate the work of the groups.

Suzy Ruder

The students in Suzy Ruder's fourth-period Freshman Basic English class, a lot more boys than girls, gradually drift into the classroom. They show, through their ripped jeans, their detached stares, and their leisurely gait, that they are alienated from the scholarly pursuits of high school.

Indeed, many of these kids have known each other for a long time, having been tracked together at the bottom of their classes since elementary school. They are very familiar with the school game: they have been losing at it for many years.

But today, they have come to class ready to work. Everyone has remembered to bring two items: the book their literature circle group is reading and their filled-out role sheets (for discussion director, literary luminary, word wizard, and a new role invented by their teacher, creative connector). Because they know that their circles are meeting today, the kids immediately begin pushing desks into groups. Ms. R doesn't need to issue any commands, she just helps move chairs. After a few minutes of settling, joking, and poking, the groups settle down to work. For the next thirty-five or forty minutes, five student-led groups engage in informal, energetic, natural conversations about books.

The discussion director convenes each group, usually by tossing out an open-ended query along the lines of, What did you think about last night's reading? Was anyone else surprised when . . ? What do you think will happen next? Joanne is the discussion director for a group that's reading Robert Newton Peck's coming-of-age novel *A Day No Pigs Would Die*. The group members have just read the first few chapters, and Joanne asks, "Why didn't his father hit him for skipping school?" The kids kick this idea around halfheartedly for a moment, but it is Joanne's next question that opens a lively chat: "Have you ever had any stitches like the boy gets in the book?" This spurs a brisk, if gruesome, pooling of prior knowledge about stitches. Since, as this particular book develops, wounding and killing are very much at the center of the story, the kids' discussion of their own past wounds sets the stage for later, deeper talk.

Kids play their individual, daily-rotating roles in an interwoven, spontaneous, and unpredictable pattern. Bill, the word wizard for the *Pigs* group, has brought "rooted," "goiter," "butternut," and "birthsop" as the words of the day. The first three he has been able to locate and copy from the dictionary, but the last was unfindable. Opening their books to the page in question, the group looks at the word in the context of the chapter, where its relation to pig breeding becomes clear. Nisreen, the literary luminary, has picked several passages to read aloud, one because she finds it "moody," another because it's "exciting," and a third because, she explains, "it has good ideas." People listen and talk naturally about their responses to the passages. Pete, the creative connector, asks the group members if they have ever gotten into trouble with their parents as the protagonist does for wrecking his mother's garden. Pete shares a story of getting "yelled at" by his mother, and gets a knowing, empathic hearing from the group.

Around the room, other groups are talking about other books, but the pattern is the same. The discussion director starts things off, and sometimes it takes several questions or several people's responses to get a continuing, natural-feeling discussion going. But it usually happens. As the group gains momentum, the other role players weigh in, contributing their piece to the puzzle—either when their role is cued naturally by the discussion or when the discussion director calls on them. "What was your picture, Beth?" he might ask, and then the other members would each offer a speculative interpretation of Beth's illustration before leaving her the final (and definitive) word. Different groups have developed different styles for getting the work done, and Ms. R has made it clear that "digressions" sparked by the ideas in the books are not wrong but welcome.

While the kids are working, Suzy circulates through the room, stopping to sit in on each group for perhaps five minutes. Mostly she listens while she's there, occasionally jotting a discreet note for a student's evaluation records. Sometimes she will answer questions of fact or even offer an opinion, but her main goal is to keep the process running smoothly, not to "teach" the books. Today, Suzy is especially interested in seeing how kids do with the new role—creative connector—she has introduced. As she visits different groups, she is happy to see that kids are picking up on the role's explicit invitation to associative thinking. Many of today's connectors begin their contributions by saying, "This part of the book reminded me of . . ." and then taking the text out into the rest of their experience, to the wider world. Suzy is pleased for her students, but she has no idea now that within a few months, dozens of teachers around Chicago will be using her connector role with kids ranging from primary grades through college.

A New Kind of Reading Group

Literature circles turn traditional reading instruction upside down in almost every dimension. The students, not the teacher, pick the readings and make the daily assignments. Everyone doesn't read the same book at the same time. If there are twenty-five students in the class, there might be five, six, or seven different groups meeting at once, each reading a different book. These groups are temporary and are formed on the basis of students' mutual interest in a particular book. The reading materials aren't short, linguistically controlled basal stories or content-overloaded textbook chapters, but real, whole, unabridged books—children's, young adult, or classic literature or biography, history, or science. Kids develop and pursue their own discussion topics, instead of answering textbook study questions or submitting to a teacher's "gentle inquisition." The teacher's role has shifted from the presenter/questioner at the center of attention to an unobtrusive, quiet facilitator. In this classroom structure, the students are the ones making the choices, raising the questions, doing the talking, and making the meaning.

About This Book

This book is designed, above all, to be practical for teachers. Its main goals are:

- To explain clearly what literature circles are.
- To help you get circles started with your students.
- To solve the common management problems that may arise.
- To offer lots of variations that may suit your students, your situation, and your style.
- To help you extend lit circles into a wide range of studies across the curriculum.

This book addresses educators across a very wide span of grade levels, from primary through college. How can this be possible? How can one book be practical for people working with such disparate learners? That it can is because literature circles is one of those very few "big ideas" that genuinely applies to *all of us who teach*. I believe—and I trust this book will prove—that the basic structure of literature circles, like most truly important educational concepts, reaches authentically across grade levels. That means that all the key organizational issues, patterns, procedures, and materials will be similar and translatable across all levels of schooling.

I am also encouraged to write a kindergarten-through-college book because this has been the real-life mixture of our literature circles network group here in Chicago. The chapters that follow draw heavily on the experiences, stories, and words of about twenty literature circle veterans, a sparkling and diverse group of elementary, middle, secondary, and college teachers who have been developing and sharing ideas for several years. We hail from a wide range of schools in Chicago and around the Midwest—from all-minority inner-city classrooms to affluent suburban schools to technical and liberal arts colleges, and everything in between. As we have gathered and talked over the years, we have repeatedly found that wonderful insights, solutions, and management ideas for any classroom can come from *any other grade level.* Originally, Suzy Ruder invented the role of connector specifically for her basic-track high school kids. But once Suzy shared that role with our group, it immediately got appropriated, reworked, and recreated. Now, connectors are working in scores of classrooms from kindergarten through college. So, if you read this book with an eye for analogies and metaphors, as well as for direct applications, you'll find translatable ideas from teachers of all levels.

Many of this book's special contributors are also graduates of the Walloon Institute and serve as teacher-consultants in the Illinois Writing Project. In addition to working in their own classrooms, these teacher-leaders offer workshops and demonstrations for colleagues in their own districts and beyond. Their generosity in sharing their ideas with me—and, through this book, with you—is typical of their professional commitment and leadership.

A Natural Structure

Just like Karen, Marianne, and Suzy's students, readers love to talk. Readers need to talk. And readers *do* talk. All across this country, people who read find ways of connecting with other readers—folks who have read the same book or books by the same author or books in the same genre or books completely unrelated. Every day, tens of thousands of American adults gather voluntarily in book discussion groups—meeting in church basements, bookstores, community centers, retirement homes, and private houses—to talk about their reading. Indeed, some readers will even settle for talking about books with nonreaders, as long as they'll sit still and listen. This need to share our responses to books is so automatic that we often don't recognize its insistent power.

Have you ever had this experience? You have just finished reading a wonderful book, and you feel the immediate urge to tell someone about it. There's no one around who's read the same book, but that doesn't stop you. You grab someone, often a spouse, coworker, or good friend—whoever's handy. You corner them in the kitchen or by the water cooler, and you commence a breathless account of your reading. In your enthusiasm, you may back your friend up against the refrigerator or the bulletin board as you pepper them with details, feelings, events from the book. If you have the book in hand, you might even find yourself reading a favorite passage aloud. "Isn't that great?" you ask. Usually, if these conscripted audiences love us, they will respond patiently, saying "uh-huh," "oh, really," "how nice" in the appropriate gaps as we ramble on. When we're done, we usually make them promise to read the book, and (if only to end the barrage) they often agree. And if those of us who occasionally perpetrate these literary ambushes ever stopped to think about it, we would probably recognize that our own understanding of the book we have just talked about has been significantly deepened by the conversation—or monologue—we've just had.

The uses of these one-sided conversations, quite obviously, are mainly for the reader. Readers need to talk. The same is true for kids in school. For too long, we've treated school reading as a solitary, internal, somewhat lonely act. We haven't provided opportunities for kids just to read, just to react, to behave like normal real-world readers who need to express, effuse, emote, think, and weigh during and after reading. We've asked kids to bottle up their responses, and in doing so we have blocked the pathway that leads upward from responding to analyzing and evaluating.

Opening the Door to Natural Book Talk in Classrooms

Two of the most important promising ideas in education today are *collaborative learning* and *independent reading.* Though neither of these ideas is new, both have reemerged with new urgency and clarity amid the current school reform movement.

All across the country, teachers are discovering the power of collaborative grouping for learning across the curriculum. Major reports from virtually every teaching field, from the key professional societies and research centers, have formally defined collaborative learning as a key ingredient of "best educational practice" (Zemelman, Daniels, and Hyde 1993). The traditional, individualistic classroom, with kids sitting quietly in rows of seats doing their solitary work, is gradually disappearing. Using models from pioneers like David and Roger Johnson and William Glasser, teachers from kindergarten through college are deploying their students in a rich array of collaborative and cooperative structures. Research—some of it reaching back twenty years or more—shows solid achievement gains when kids work in such teams across the curriculum (Johnson, Johnson, Holubec, and Roy 1991). Just as American industry has discovered the power of "quality circles" in the factory and the office, educators have rediscovered the educational power of collaboration in the classroom.

Sadly, some abuses of cooperative learning do exist—corruptions that turn student groups into competitive teams memorizing trivial bits of the same old curriculum. Because of these degradations, our terminology has begun to change: today, the term "cooperative learning" is increasingly identified with the more structured, memorization-oriented, teacher-dominated kinds of group work, while "collaborative learning" defines the more open-ended and student-centered kinds of inquiry. Though this book still uses the two terms interchangeably, it is the original collaborative ideal of student-initiated inquiry that we embrace.

Small groups can be efficient, energizing, sometimes almost magical structures for learning. Why are they so powerful? The limited size invites—almost compels—every individual to be an active participant in sharing ideas and constructing interpretations. When there are only three or four people in a group, each person's careful listening and frequent sharing are necessary for the group to function; everyone automatically has a degree of responsibility and investment. This is quite unlike the situation in large-group discussions, where one person speaks and perhaps thirty others wait for their widely scattered turns to join in.

But even more important than the benefits of efficient communication and tangible products, genuine collaborative learning brings to our classrooms the long-neglected values of democracy, community, and shared responsibility. When structured carefully and implemented authentically, cooperative learning invites students to set their own goals, pursue their own questions, conduct their own inquiries. Unlike the traditional teacher-centered, convergent model of education, where all activities are aimed at a single predetermined outcome, cooperative learning is open-ended and student-centered.

During the past fifteen years, research has also been accumulating about the importance of students' independent reading experiences, of children's selecting and reading their own books. The Center for the Study of Reading reports that the single factor most strongly associated with reading achievement—more than socioeconomic status or any instructional approach—is independent reading (Anderson, Wilson, and Fielding 1988). In other words, kids who read on their own, who read books they have chosen for themselves, become the strongest readers. The message is clear: kids should be reading—which means choosing, responding to, talking about, and keeping records of—far more books than any one teacher could ever assign or monitor.

But in school we've traditionally allowed kids little choice or ownership of their reading, instead marching them through an endless lockstep series of teacher-selected and teacher-controlled readings. Mostly, this reading has been done in basal readers, literature anthologies, or fact-stuffed textbooks, with a focus on memorizing details, not on getting the big picture. Ironically, as a result of this prevalent microcomprehension approach, kids actually read rather little—poring over relatively few densely packed pages of artificial school-made text, rather than tearing through stacks of whole, real books. The result: kids don't get enough practice with reading to get good at it—or to like it. We Americans may wring our hands about having a nation of nonreaders, but traditional school reading programs are virtually *designed* to ensure that kids never voluntarily pick up a book once they graduate.

Collaborating on Reading

Here in Chicago, the first teacher to consciously combine these two ideas—independent reading and cooperative learning—was Becky Abraham Searle. Back in 1981, Becky was teaching a multiage 4–5–6 classroom at Virginia Lake School in Palatine. Among her older children there were many high-achieving readers who quickly burned through all the materials in the district's mandated basal program. When Becky requested additional reading materials from the district and a set of seventh-grade workbooks was delivered, she knew she had to try something else. Since she had already been experimenting with cooperative learning (years later she would study with the Johnsons and become a cooperative learning workshop leader), it seemed natural to Becky to form these voracious readers into literature discussion groups. Spending some book-club points, she assembled sets of Jean George's *Julie of the Wolves* and Robert Newton Peck's *A Day No Pigs Would Die* and set the kids to reading. But while the students did enthusiastically read the books, the discussions dragged and the kids relied on Becky too much for guidance and structure. She wanted them to run their own group discussions, wanted to get herself out of the middle of their conversations. So Becky devised four simple role sheets that gave each group member a task: discussion director, literary luminary, vocabulary enricher, and process checker. Using and rotating these roles, Becky found that students had deeper, more independent, more self-sustaining discussions. After a few cycles of role-structured discussions, she withdrew the role sheets and invited students to record their ideas and questions in response logs, which turned out to support the reading process and the group meetings much as the role sheets had. It's quite a credit to Becky's invention that today her versions of literature circles (and especially her role sheets) are being shared, used, revised, and improvised on by teachers all across North America.

Defining Literature Circles

So two potent ideas—independent reading and cooperative learning—come together in the elegant and exciting classroom activity called literature circles. As we have seen, some great teachers like Becky Abraham Searle and Karen Smith had already figured out this basic structure back in the early 1980s. Since then, Jerome Harste, Kathy Short, and Carolyn Burke (1988) and Ralph Peterson and Maryann Eeds (1990) have published descriptions offering teachers around the country basic models to experiment with. Kathy Short and Kathryn Mitchell Pierce's collection of essays (1992) provides a whole volume of examples, ways in which teachers have organized literature discussion groups in a wide variety of classrooms. Lucy Calkins (1986), Shelley Harwayne (1992), and Regie Routman (1991) have all contributed variations of book clubs and other kid-led reading groups that are similar in spirit and function.

Here in the Midwest, our loosely knit team of teachers has been developing our own version of literature circles for almost fifteen years, combining local inventions like Becky Searle's role sheets with national models appearing in the literature. Here, we've been especially concerned with the issues of management, the preparation of students, and enacting the principles of group dynamics. Perhaps our most unique and important contribution has been to infuse the key formal elements of collaborative learning into our model—particularly through the varied roles we've devised for orienting students and running newly formed lit circles groups. Most of the rest of this book explains how and why we've evolved into setting up and running literature circles the way we do.

Do we think our model is better? Certainly not. We are genuinely dazzled and impressed by the diverse ways that other teachers around the country have created and supported literature discussion groups. But we do believe we have a some special contributions to make. We think our model makes it easier and safer for more kids (and more teachers) to try literature circles. We have developed a particularly effective way of getting started, a way of using role sheets to create a quick, successful implementation of student-led discussion groups in the classroom. We have also developed a variety of structures and procedures for managing literature circles over the long run, strategies that solidify and deepen the role this special activity can play in a balanced curriculum across the grade levels.

Other proponents of literature circles can and do take issue with some of our approaches; in some quarters, the use of "transitional" devices like our role sheets is controversial. We will have more to say about such debates later on. But for now we'll simply assert that our overarching goal is to "grow the club"—to enlarge the number of classrooms in which teachers can comfortably reallocate big chunks of class time to genuine student-led small-group discussions. And if that's the result, we're happy.

So what is distinctive about our version of literature circles? Here's our current definition:

> *Literature circles are small, temporary discussion groups who have chosen to read the same story, poem, article, or book. While reading each group-determined portion of the text (either in or outside of class), each member prepares to take specific responsibilities in the upcoming discussion, and everyone comes to the group with the notes needed to help perform that job. The circles have regular meetings, with discussion roles rotating each session. When they finish a book, the circle members plan a way to share highlights of their reading with the wider community; then they trade members with other finishing groups, select more reading, and move into a new cycle. Once readers can successfully conduct their own wide-ranging, self-sustaining discussions, formal discussion roles may be dropped.*

Obviously, very similar kinds of reading discussion groups have probably been around outside of schools since shortly after the invention of print. Every day, all across America, citizens attend voluntary book discussion groups that operate in a parallel format, meeting regularly in homes or community centers. Sometimes these groups have a single, ongoing leader, and sometimes leadership rotates among members; sometimes these groups are abetted by a local bookstore, senior center, community house, or other institution, and sometimes they operate independently.

But no matter how natural and widespread this kind of book-talk may be in the outside world, in schools reader-run discussions have been rare. Indeed, the formalized, in-school version of this activity is barely a decade old. But it is spreading fast: today, there are thousands of innovative teachers across the country experimenting with lit circles, tapping and exploring the potential of this powerful structure. Here in Chicago, most teachers who try literature circles are amazed that they "work" right away. While refinements and variations can go on for years, the "basic installation" of the structure is fairly quick and fail-safe. Unlike some other student-centered classroom methods, which are very complex and tricky to implement, literature circles usually succeed immediately. And that, we believe, is simply because well-structured literature circles simply re-create a basic, natural, and comfortable human structure for interacting around books and ideas.

Kids' Reactions

Of course, the main thing that pleases and encourages teachers who have just begun with literature circles is the way kids, like these fourth graders, respond right from the start:

> Lit circles are really fun! Lit circles are very neat. They are very, very awesome. Lit circles are very complicated though. First you pick a book. Then you decide were to read up to. Next you read up to that page and then you discusse the part that you read. Do that three times and then you do an awesome project then present them to the class. Like I told you lit circles are very fun. You should try a lit circle today. Trust me.

> Every Mondays & Fridays, we get into a group called the liturature groups. It is good for me because if we didn't have it, I wouldn't be reading at all! I also like it because we get to discuss the book and compare how it relates to peoples (our) lives. My favorite book in the liturature groups is the *Family Under a Bridge*. It was sad, and one of my friends said it almost made her cry. We all have jobs. (Diffrent ones.) Literary luminary (LL), discussion director (DD), process checker (PC) and vocab enricher (VE). I love liturature

groups because of the jobs too. My teacher gets us into reading and WE LOVE IT!!!!!

I am glad that our class does lit circles. It is fun reading books and sharing them. It is also fun doing the projects after we read the books. A lit circle is when three or more kids are asked to read a book. We devide the book in to different parts. After each part we get in our group and talk about it. When we are done we do a project together. Lit circles are an awesome way to read a book. It is fun to read a book and talk about it with your friends. You should try it some time with your friends.

Jay Sharma, one of Kathy Effinger's eighth-grade students in Hinsdale, Illinois, didn't think lit circles were a very good idea at first:

When I first learned that we would be reading books in class and discussing them with other children I thought the idea was too complicated and stood a very small chance of being successful. Contrary to what I first thought, when the group got together for the first time we organized very quickly and I was anxiously awaiting the next meeting. All of our discussions were to the point and all of the group did their assignments and participated in the discussions. The discussion, mostly the discussion director's and literary luminary's jobs, sparked many conversations and arguments about what the author meant and much was learned from this.

The Chocolate War was very well-written as well as interesting. The setting and the characters I could relate to, being an adolescent and almost high school student, and I was eager to find out how they would face the conflicts and dilemmas throughout the book. The only part I found unrealistic was how the school had such little discipline but was a Catholic school. The highlight of the time our group worked together was the final project. We spent close to two and a half hours putting together a minature (and extremely out of proportion) Trinity school and the field surrounding it. Without any adult help we became organized and produced a project both detailed and sturdy with time to spare. I was very impressed at how we worked together on this project and unit arguing and with every person doing their share.

Teachers Talk

The delight is not confined to students. Literature circles free teachers to take a more natural, enjoyable partner role in the classroom community. They are invited by the very nature of the structure to leave behind the position of taskmaster/teller and become a fellow reader, a coach, and a colleague. This, evidently, is a feeling that many teachers like:

Kristen Overcash, Fifth-Grade Teacher

I can't believe these kids! They're amazing! We're finally doing literature circles. I kept putting it off and I finally realized why—I don't like to shut up and let the kids run their own discussions. I'm really good at backing off during writing time, but I just love to be the discussion director in reading. Anyway, I'm learning to shut up and they're saying things like—"Why do you think the author had this character do that?" or "What from the book makes you think that? Can you take it back to the text?" or "Do you think that character is very realistic? He's just all bad." It's so cool. They really work at pulling everyone into the discussion. They're kind and thoughtful— unless someone comes to the circle unprepared—in which case they're harder on one another than I ever am on them. And when I try to interrupt (which really isn't too often), they don't let me get involved for long before they send me away. (They're really good at seeing when I'm about to cross the line from just having something interesting to contribute to taking over.) I never have to get them back on task, they're *so* involved in what they're doing. Thank you, lit circles! It means a lot to me to see my students doing something like this. It just blows my mind that they can do so much if you just guide them and then let them go.

Donna Stupple, High School English

When I first heard about literature circles I liked the idea, because it fit in with the kind of changes I was experimenting with in my classes: honest collaborative work (not seat work in groups, I mean); more reader response; more varied tasks with at least some instructional time on "invisible skills" like how you work in groups, different discussion roles, etc.; and maybe most important, decentralizing my classroom. Besides the fact that the kids worked with each other in extended, real ways, so did I. This literature circle structure forced me to be a resource person because that was the only role I could have in the midst of all the activity. I have repeated the strategy (new variations, of course—I'm too old to get prudent now!) with similar success every time. By success I don't necessarily mean complete understanding of the text; I mean an atmosphere in the classroom and an attitude that we're all kind of "rummaging" around for meaning together.

Donna Irmis, Sixth-Grade Teacher
I've been experimenting with literature circles in my sixth-grade class. To make certain the kids actually prepare, I collect their role sheets each time. I'm so glad I've done this. . . . It's been fascinating to see their drawings. They've chosen vocab words wisely, pointing up rich language in all cases. However, the most intriguing papers to read have been the connectors. These kids have made wonderful, varied, far-flung, and surprising associations. It's like a little window into their minds. One example is the kid who connected *The Hobbit* with American Indian myths, and compared the coyote and the swallowing monster to a ride at Epcot Center. I do think that adolescents need to have some space, with guidance. These circles provide that. It sure is fun experimenting. I can't wait until next fall when I'll have sixty kids for reading, language arts, and social studies. With all this stimulation, I keep thinking up ideas for next year!

Ingredients

Every day, in classrooms all across America, most students meet in some kind of small groups to work on reading. These groups use a wide variety of structures, ranging from traditional teacher-dominated round-robin reading all the way to what Becky Abraham Searle's and Marianne Flanagan's kids are doing. Unfortunately, the growing popularity of literature circles (or book clubs, or readers groups) has led, in a few places, to the superficial renaming of old-style skill-oriented basal reading groups as literature circles. While this kind of "word magic" is not unusual in education, it does cloud the picture for dedicated teachers who are trying to deeply understand and fully implement the real thing. "Literature circles" is not just a trendy label for *any* kind of small-group reading lesson—it stands for a sophisticated fusion of collaborative learning with independent reading, in the framework of reader response theory. The structure—and the teachers who use it—deserve truth-in-labeling.

Therefore, at the risk of flirting with orthodoxy, it is important to explain the differences here. What makes a genuine literature circle? What are the distinctive features of this special structure? While some of the defining ingredients of literature circles may be intentionally omitted when students are first learning the activity or when the group is applying lit circles to some mandated curriculum, authentic and mature literature circles will manifest most or all of these key features:

1. Students *choose* their own reading materials.
2. *Small temporary groups* are formed, based on book choice.
3. Different groups read *different books*.
4. Groups meet on a *regular, predictable schedule* to discuss their reading.
5. Kids use written or drawn *notes* to guide both their reading and discussion.
6. Discussion *topics come from the students*.
7. Group meetings aim to be *open, natural conversations about books*, so personal connections, digressions, and open-ended questions are welcome.
8. In newly forming groups, students play a rotating assortment of task *roles*.
9. The teacher serves as a *facilitator*, not a group member or instructor.
10. Evaluation is by *teacher observation and student self-evaluation*.
11. A spirit of *playfulness and fun* pervades the room.
12. When books are finished, *readers share with their classmates*, and then *new groups form* around new reading choices.

1. Children choose their own reading materials

Student choice tops the list, because the deepest spirit of literature circles comes from independent reading. One of the gravest shortcomings of school reading programs is that assignments, choices, texts to read, are usually all controlled by the teacher. This contrasts sharply with what we know of good home-based teaching, where parents intuitively provide kids with choices in their reading and discussion of books. Parents do not snuggle up to their offspring at story time and then announce: "It's October 19, so today the curriculum says we have to cover *Goodnight Moon.*" Caring parents simply say, "What do you want to read?" and even if the child selects the same book for the tenth night in a row or a book that's too hard or too easy for her to understand, the parent still lets the kid lead. What parents know in their hearts, even if they cannot explain it, is that you can't fall in love with books that someone stuffs down your throat. For reading to become a lifelong habit and a deeply owned skill, it has to be voluntary, anchored in feelings of pleasure and power.

In the classroom, teachers who really want to meet this need for genuine choice and self-direction must provide two kinds of independent reading: time for *individuals,* through structures like sustained silent reading (SSR) and reading workshop (see Chapter 9); and time for independent reading in *groups,* as when kids select, read, and discuss books in literature circles.

2. Small temporary groups are formed, based on book choice

Literature circle groups are formed around several people's shared desire to read the same book or article—not by reading level, ability grouping, teacher assignment, or curriculum mandate. These groups are temporary and task oriented. They often mix children of different "abilities." Once they have finished their job—reading and discussing a book of common interest—the group disbands and individual members find their way into new, different groups by picking their next book. Group size can range from two to six, although the optimum seems to be four or five. This number guarantees a variety of perspectives on the text, a range of responses that enlivens discussion, and the option of parceling out several quite different reading and discussion roles.

In real schools, our ideals of book choice and group formation are sometimes compromised. To begin with, kids will not be picking from all the books in the world, but from those fairly handy in the classroom or the school or the local public library. The teacher may not be able to provide enough copies of a chosen book, and then kids will have to read their second or third choice instead. When teachers are just starting a class off with literature circles, they may decide to limit students' choices to a few books—or even assign a single title to all groups—in order to focus students on learning the structure. Sometimes, parents or teachers may limit the choices by refusing to let kids read books they consider inappropriate.

There may also be compromises or imperfections in the formation of groups. Of course, smart teachers know that many kids will pick books not out of genuine curiosity, but to create a group of their friends. But these teachers also realize that as long as kids do the reading, invest in the conversation, get into the book, this is not a problem. Students tend to act exactly like adult book discussion groups in our culture do—a group of people first decide that they want to be together, and then they pick some books as the centerpiece of their gathering. Other teachers have kids pick books through secret ballots that ensure a more authentic expression of interest in particular books. Sometimes teachers have to mediate, guide, and counsel in order to get groups formed and make things come out even. Groups may have to include some kids who are reading a first-choice title and others for whom it's a backup or secondary choice. Some teachers feel that in order to get a good, rich discussion going it is important to have three or four people in a group, so they try to talk kids out of pairs, even if that's the true first-choice grouping. While all these compromises may not be ideal, they are realistic. Even as teachers give classroom time to creating the groups and solving the difficulties democratically, they are explicitly demonstrating their commitment to honor student choice and make it work.

3. Different groups read different books

Obviously, when kids (or adults) are given a genuine choice of what to read, not everyone will pick the same book. More and more teachers realize that this variety is long overdue. In traditional American schools, virtually every single book, article, story, text, poem, chapter, novel, and play that students read throughout their first twelve or thirteen years is assigned by a teacher, dictated by the curriculum, and backed by the authority of grades. Now, this everybody-reads-the-same-thing approach isn't always bad. After all, it can be very helpful to be part of a wider community that has all read the same text, giving readers a wide range of different responses to hear and ponder.

However, our best research on the development of readers is very clear: assignments are not enough. Children need a mixture, a balance between teacher-chosen and self-selected materials (Zemelman, Daniels, and Hyde 1993). They need substantive opportunities to develop and pursue their own tastes, curiosities, and enthusiasms in the world of books. In fact, choice is actually a matter of educational standards and rigor. Students must learn to take full responsibility for locating, selecting, and pursuing books, rather than always expecting teachers or other adults to choose for them. Since choice is an integral component of literate behavior, if we don't require students to be constantly assigning reading to themselves, we have set our educational standards far too low and are nurturing dependency and helplessness. By providing structures and schedules to promote student-chosen reading experience at all levels, activities like literature circles, reading workshop, and sustained silent reading offer a way to redress our schools' dangerous imbalance between assigned and independent reading.

4. Groups meet on a regular, predictable schedule

In order to work most effectively, literature circles must be regularly scheduled—not as an occasional "treat," but continuously throughout the school year. If LCs are introduced as a one-time-only special event, teachers and kids will just have time to learn the procedures, go through one book (probably a bit mechanically, since the first time through is always a mixture of learning the process and discussing the book), and then quit just when the real payoff is in view. Lit circles hit their stride when everyone has tried all the roles, internalized the norms, and warmed up as readers. Teachers need to see this as a long-term classroom investment: literature circles require a modest "down payment" of time for training, but once they're installed in your portfolio of strategies, they pay big dividends in the reading program all year long.

The daily and weekly meeting schedules are important, too. Any lit circle session needs a good chunk of time—even with the youngest or most distractible kids anything less than twenty minutes doesn't allow the possibility for a natural conversation to open up. When sessions are too short, kids tend to rush mechanically through their roles, and the session becomes a kind of cooperative oral workbook with everyone hurrying to jump over each hurdle in the allotted time. For older kids and more focused groups, thirty minutes is a healthy chunk of time, while forty-five minutes will be welcomed and well used by lit circle veterans.

Predictability is another factor. If kids are going to self-assign parts of a book, read with purpose, make notes on a role sheet or in their reading log, and come to class ready to play their part in the discussion, they need a sensible, predictable schedule. Circles can meet every day, with kids doing the reading each night and changing roles daily. Or groups can meet every second or third day, allowing time for kids to read bigger chunks of text between meetings (and allowing the teacher to slide in some other curriculum in the intervening days). Some teachers have kids do their reading and prepare their notes on nonmeeting days during the same class time that the circles otherwise meet. This kind of schedule is especially helpful in the training stages or for kids who don't do well reading their books as homework. This pattern also allows the teacher to support students' reading, circulating to go over their role sheets, to model open-ended questions, to reassure kids that their own real responses are truly invited.

5. Kids use written or drawn notes to guide both their reading and discussion

Writing and drawing play a vital role in all stages of literature circles. During reading, the role sheets encourage readers to stop and use prose or drawings to capture, record, crystalize, and play with their thinking and responses to the text. This kind of writing is open-ended and personal; it invites kids to generate extended, original language, not to jot "correct" phrases in response to workbook blanks or story-starter prompts. Later, when members come to the group, they use their own writings as a starting place for conversation and sharing. In groups that have "graduated" from the structured role sheets, reading logs take over the writing/drawing function, serving as a repository of readers' responses to their reading. When the group gathers, these reading logs, too, are a source ready to be drawn upon for discussion questions and ideas. When a book is completed, groups or individuals typically engage in a sharing project as a way of synthesizing the reading for themselves and extending its reach to a wider audience. Sometimes such projects involve more formal, polished, audience-centered kinds of writing, such as a book review, a "missing chapter" of the book, a book poster, or a readers theater script. Across the whole cycle of a literature circle, then, writing and drawing are used to drive—and to record—the meaning constructed and the ideas shared.

6. Discussion topics come from the students

One of the signal features of literature circles is that *kids develop their own discussion topics* and bring them to the group. The teacher does not provide the questions, whether verbally, on worksheets, or in study guides. Now it may happen (and often does) that the topics kids come up with match the ones the teacher would have asked. But ownership makes a big difference: this way, students are in charge of their thinking and discussion.

Sometimes people mistake this element of literature circles as a kind of "permissiveness." But this is not a matter of "letting" kids choose their own discussion topics, or "allowing" or "permitting" them to do so. On the contrary, in literature circles, we *require* that students find and develop their own topics for discussion. Unlike the traditional classroom, in which teachers have lower expectations and therefore supply all discussion topics, in literature circles our standards are much higher. In these challenging discussion groups, kids must perform all the acts that real, mature readers do—from picking their own books to making their own assignments to selecting issues for discussion, all the way through to sharing and expressing their views of the book to fellow readers. After all, if kids never practice digging the big ideas out of texts themselves and always have teachers doing it for them, how can they ever achieve literary and intellectual independence?

7. Group meetings aim to be open, natural conversations

Schools have traditionally favored convergent, objective questions—tasks in which the answers are fact based and verifiably "correct." In literature circles, while we are always interested in the details of what we read and always take care to build our interpretations on a close reading of the text, we begin our conversations with personal response. We connect with one another around divergent, open-ended, interpretive questions—questions of value:

Does this book seem true to life?
How is this character like me?
Does this family remind me of my own?
If faced with this kind of choice, what would I do?
Could the people in this book have risen above their circumstances?

We take seriously the literary theory of reader response, which says that students cannot effectively move to the level of analysis until they have worked through, processed, savored, shared their personal response (Rosenblatt 1938).

But more than this—and here I part company with some other proponents of literature groups—much of the time, *sharing responses is enough.* Rather than forcing students onward to an explicit structural analysis of the literary components of the work, it's often fine to say: "That was great. Let's read another one." After all, if students have worked through a book together—sharing their views from a variety of angles, listening to selected passages read aloud, looking at one another's drawings, talking over particular vocabulary, connecting the work to their own lives, searching out questions of common interest among peers—is not the writer's craft being studied in a very deep, though implicit, way?

Though some teachers do seek ways to infuse literary terminology and analytical procedures into their literature circles, I do not see this as one of the structure's defining ingredients. Indeed, the distinctive value of literature circles is that it enacts another paradigm of learning. It is based on a faith in self-directed practice. Literature circles embody the idea that kids learn to read mainly by reading and to write mainly by writing and by doing so in a supportive, literate community. Of course we trust that kids' appreciation of the author's craft will grow as they read more and more and that their own writing will, over time, reflect the deep, unconscious influences of all they have read. But the starting point, the way in, and the base for everything is "just reading" and "just responding" to lots and lots of books.

8. In newly forming groups, students play a rotating assortment of task roles

One of the key insights of collaborative learning experts like the Johnsons, William Glasser, and others is the need for clear tasks and roles in a group. Unfortunately, most American schoolchildren are still mainly socialized to a competitive, individualistic model of behavior in school, so they may arrive at structures like lit circles relatively unprepared to cooperate in a comfortable and productive way. Therefore, we have to help them acquire the social skills of collaboration first. One of the key mechanisms for making cooperation work in all sorts of groups is assigning specific, structured roles to the different group members. This way, each person has a special, individual responsibility, a job to do, a piece of the puzzle to contribute if the group is to succeed.

When we fuse this idea with research on reading comprehension, the importance of assigning group roles deepens. We now understand that the old way of assigning texts—"read this by Friday"—sets the stage for poor understanding. Current reading theory stresses the importance of helping kids to activate their prior knowledge about a topic or author, to set purposes for reading, to make predictions, and to be constantly "interrogating the text" for clarity and meaning. When everyone in class is reading the same book, teachers can use a whole range of elegant strategies to help kids accomplish these cognitive tasks. But how do we provide this support before and during reading when kids are reading *different* books in cooperative groups? Certainly not by sending the teacher around to conduct prereading activities group by group! Instead, we use the device of the role sheets, not just to structure responsibilities during the eventual group meeting, but to guide kids' thinking while they read.

In Chapter 5 is an assortment of roles that teachers in our network have developed and used, along with some samples of the sheets adapted to different grade levels. These basic roles are designed to invite different cognitive perspectives on a text (drawing a response, reading a passage aloud, debating interpretations, connecting to one's own life, creating a summary, tracking the scene, focusing on words, tuning in to one character). We have found that successful roles are a curious mixture of structure and openness. The best ones closely specify the process and focus of kids' jobs but *not the content.* Good roles are always open-ended—the opposite of the usual correct-answer worksheets, workbooks, and study questions.

Rotating the roles is important, too. In this way everyone gets to look at the story from a little bit different angle each day, gradually internalizing the perspectives of the illustrator, the literary luminary, etc. Students (or adults) who have done literature circles for any length of time usually report that they have internalized all the roles they have played and that now when they read they unconsciously—and irrepressibly—think in terms not just of the one role they happen to have today, but all the roles they have played over time. This, of course, can be a signal to the teacher either to introduce some different roles or to start phasing out the role sheets in favor of an open-ended reading journal. When kids have internalized the perspectives of sophisticated, multipurposeful readers, they are ready to have natural conversations about books without the role sheets, using just their memories and notes jotted in a personal response log.

9. *The teacher serves as a facilitator*

The teacher's main job in literature circles is to *not teach,* at least in the traditional sense of the term. For this special student-centered classroom activity, we must bring back, with pride and respect, the much abused term *facilitator,* taken from the work of Carl Rogers (another whole language progenitor whose ideas are today being validated in classrooms around the country). As the many stories in Chapters 6 and 7 show, the teacher's work in literature circles is complex, artful, and absolutely essential. It just doesn't happen to include any lecturing, telling, or advising. (None of this means, of course, that at other times of the day the teacher can't lecture or otherwise "really teach." See Chapter 9 for more on this.) But now, during literature circles, most of the teacher's work is organizational, managerial, and logistical. Teachers collect sets of good books, help groups to form, visit and observe group meetings, confer with kids or groups who struggle, orchestrate sharing sessions, keep records, make assessment notes, and collect still more books.

In some literature circle classrooms, teachers also elect to play another key role: that of fellow reader. They join a group not as the teacher but as an equal, reading right along with kids a book they haven't previously read—and want to read. Obviously, teachers can only make this choice when the room's other lit circles are running smoothly enough that they can stay in one group over a couple of weeks' time. A teacher's becoming a fellow reader, honestly reading, responding, predicting, and sharing meaning-making processes right along with the students, offers a radically different and powerful demonstration of how mature readers really think.

Perhaps the one element most grievously lacking in the experience of most American schoolchildren is regularly seeing a mature adult reader connecting with books, constructing meaning, talking about the thinking process, or sharing literary tastes. Teachers are sometimes threatened by this mandate to demonstrate, assuming that a paragon of reading process, elevated literary taste, and authoritative interpretation is the goal. But this kind of modeling doesn't require perfection. On the contrary, we want kids to see how real readers really operate, which is far from neat, orderly, and tidy. Effective adult reading is a complex constructive process, full of false starts, recursions, fix-ups, dead ends, blind alleys—not to mention personal quirks, tastes, strengths, and weaknesses. It's valuable for kids to see how all these attributes of real working readers go together day after day—not to be copied, but as one sample to build on, to vary from, to improvise off. If teachers are secure enough, they can "teach" their students a great deal simply joining a group as an equal and reading a new book right along with the students.

10. Evaluation is by teacher observation and student self-evaluation

Because literature circles do not aim to "cover material" or teach specific "subskills," the evaluation methods tied to those kinds of instruction are irrelevant. For literature circles, we need high-order assessment of kids working at the whole thing, the complete, put-together outcome—which, in this case, is joining in a thoughtful small-group conversation about literature. So how do we assess a student's achievement in such a complex event? Drawing on the burgeoning research and classroom lore of "authentic assessment," we use the tools of kidwatching, narrative observational logs, performance assessment, checklists, student conferences, group interviews, video/audiotaping, and the collection in portfolios of the artifacts created by circles. Because the structure of lit circles frees teachers from being the center of attention, they actually have time to conduct some of these more qualitative forms of evaluation while circulating through the classroom.

But evaluation in literature circles is not just the job of the teacher. Just as we require that kids take responsibility for their own book selections, topic choices, role sheets, and reading assignments, we also want them involved in the record-keeping and evaluation activities of literature circles. Because self-monitoring is such a key ingredient in the reading process, it only makes sense that kids in literature circles are regularly asked to write and talk evaluatively about their own goals, roles, and performances in literature circles.

11. A spirit of playfulness and fun pervades the room

It is a tenet of much modern learning theory—especially in the field of psycholinguistics—that young children learn most everything of importance to them by *playing at it* first. Indeed, *fun* is the factor that most effectively keeps learners engaged in complex learning tasks outside of school, whether it is learning to speak one's native language or to water ski. Educators have recently come to recognize that the playful early childhood activities of "scribble writing" and "pretend reading" play a central role in the development of preschool children's literacy. Indeed, playing with books and playing with writing and drawing are not mere precursors to literacy but are real reading and writing. Similarly, the research on interaction in families, from the scaffolding work of Jerome Bruner (1961) to more recent family studies (Taylor and Dorsey-Gaines 1988; Heath 1985), shows that caring, playful adult-child relationships are crucial to nurturing learning. The "lap method," in which a parent gives a child full and loving attention and models the use of language for a real purpose, may be the most effective instructional strategy ever documented.

Teachers who implement literature circles in their classroom are re-creating for their students the kind of close, playful interaction that scaffolds learning so productively elsewhere in life. They develop their classroom as a kind of analogous family, a substitute lap, another kind of dining-room table. It's no surprise, then, that teachers are energized by literature circles, that they so often comment on how much they and their students *enjoy* the time together. And when fun is unleashed in the classroom, can learning be far behind?

12. New groups form around new reading choices

Like many groups in the nonschool world, literature circles are formed when there is a job to do together, and when the job is done, the group disbands and its members move on to other projects. This means that there is a constant mixing in the classroom, with different combinations of children being thrown together with each new book choice. From a literary point of view, this regular reshuffling of personalities and perspectives in discussion groups is enriching and challenging. With each new book comes a new set of coreaders, complete with their unique, sometimes unexpected views and interpretations.

The constant recombining of people into new groupings also enacts the principle of group dynamics whereby widespread, diffuse communication and friendship patterns in a classroom build cohesion and productivity. While it may seem more comfortable for kids to stay in the same literature circle and not switch, it is in the long-term best interest of the whole group (and the individuals it comprises) that everyone be brave and move on. Indeed, many teachers come to value this mixing phenomenon so highly that they work skillfully through book recommendations and personal persuasion to ensure that kids don't place themselves back into the same groups over and over.

At a deeper level, this regular mixing of student groups is also important because literature circles offer a model of detracking, of how heterogeneous classes can work. Even if a classroom includes wildly diverse reading levels or "academic abilities," everyone can still pick books that group them at their own level. But this kind of leveling is self-chosen, temporary, and still within a mixed class—a huge difference from the permanent, official, and involuntary segregation of most school tracking systems. Further, in lit circle classrooms, kids can (and do) switch levels; they can pick harder or easier books, depending on their interest in certain authors, topics, or genres. Teachers encourage and support this kind of risk taking and stretching. The various discussion roles allow different kinds of kids to contribute successfully. For example, a student who isn't strong on verbal analysis may still offer her group an illustration that surprises and enriches the conversation. Or a special education student who needs to have the novel read aloud to him at home can still come to a discussion group and make arresting connections between the characters and his own life. In other words, literature circles, when done well, help make ability grouping unnecessary. They show how heterogeneous, diverse student groups—including mainstreamed special education kids—can work together effectively.

A New Old Idea

For those groups of individuals who do not have occasions to talk
about what and how meanings are achieved in written materials,
important cognitive and interpretive skills which are basic to being
literate do not develop.
* —Shirley Brice Heath*

THE CLASSROOM activity we now call literature circles is a new combination of some solid, old ideas from several different fields. The name, however, is relatively new. Kathy Short and Gloria Kaufman get credit for assigning the name "literature circles" to this special kind of small-group literature discussion structure, kid-led groups that show the genuine features of cooperative learning and student-centeredness. Short wrote at length about this innovation in her 1986 dissertation, titled *Literacy as a Collaborative Experience,* which was done under Jerome Harste and Carolyn Burke at Indiana University. A couple of years later, literature circles appeared as a featured activity in Harste, Short, and Burke's excellent book *Creating Classrooms for Authors* (1988). All of these writers credit Karen Smith, our friend from Chapter 1 and now Associate Executive Director of the National Council of Teachers of English, as the original source for their ideas and structures. Here in the Chicago area, we've had a special teacher, Becky Searle of Palatine School District 15, who first introduced and shared many of the role sheets discussed in this book.

Of course, the underlying ingredients of this "new" activity turn out to be remarkably old, durable, and proven. What's really novel, after all—and genuinely valuable—is the *combination.* In a few moments, I'll sketch the origins, theories, and people that constitute the heritage of this new/old idea. But first a caution is in order.

Since its introduction to the profession less than a decade ago, the term "literature circles" has spread widely, not always with its basic features intact. Indeed, like so many other innovations in education, the name is quickly being co-opted, and "literature circles" pops up as a catchy-sounding new label for practically *any* kind of reading discussion group—even those that categorically violate the fundamental tenets of the procedure. Sadly, I have visited more than one classroom in which traditional, ability-grouped, round-robin basal reading groups have been renamed "literature circles."

Why quibble over terminology? I believe that literature circles are a deeply and inherently powerful structure. If not completely revolutionary, they are at least genuinely progressive. When implemented as they were originally conceived, literature circles have the potential to transform power relationships in the classroom, to make kids both more responsible for and more in control of their own education, to unleash lifelong readers, and to nurture a critical, personal stance toward ideas. Indeed, one of the main benefits of literature circles is that they can *replace* old, destructive skill-and-drill methods—methods exactly like the round-robin reading groups now being casually renamed and treated as "the same thing" by ill-trained teachers and cynical marketers alike. Literature circles is an idea worth not corrupting. *Outcomes*

Now, I am not being a purist. As I have already said, every good session of literature circles I've ever attended departs from the basic definition in *some* ways. Smart teachers adjust their literature circles as needed, occasionally assigning a book, or handpicking a group, or taking a more active role in guiding a discussion. In Chapters 6 and 7, there are many stories of teachers making just these kinds of adjustment in the model. However, when an activity that calls itself literature circles consistently violates *most or all* of the basic ingredients, then it is a theft. It is a theft because the misapprehension of the name undermines the spread of this valuable strategy. If people don't know what the thing really is, they can never try the real thing. And if they think the things they have always done are really the same as the latest thing, what's the reason to experiment and change? So, for all these reasons, it is valuable to look at the rich and surprisingly long history of literature circles.

History

Where did this special, powerful structure come from? Well, originally, it came from individual teachers, of course, many of whom have already been celebrated in this book. But the invention and development of literature circles was also nourished by the work of some educational theorists, thinkers, and critics, some of whom I want to recognize later in a kind of "honor roll" of progenitors. But the key ideas of literature circles also originated from certain fields of study and research—linguistics, group dynamics, literary theory, and others—which I want to discuss now. For many of these ideas, it is a return visit—they are receiving a second or third "audition" in American schools. It seems to be part of our change process that ideas keep coming back for repeated tryouts, and, if they reappear when the context is more supportive and the management issues can be dealt with, they are suddenly seen to "work" where they didn't before.

Reading-as-Thinking Research

Over the past twenty years, there has been a major and healthy shift toward seeing reading (like writing) as a complex, dynamic, and recursive cognitive process, rather than as a single, somewhat magical act (Fielding and Pearson 1994; Ogle 1987). We now understand that skillful readers use a rich variety of specific and usually unconscious thinking strategies to get ready *before reading,* to construct meaning *during reading,* and to take ideas beyond the text *after reading.* Today, we represent the steps or tasks that readers accomplish with a model like this:

before reading

> Develop motivation
> Activate prior knowledge
> Gather and organize ideas
> Develop questions
> Determine purpose and strategy
> Make predictions

during reading

> Sample the text
> Visualize text meaning
> Make connections

Confirm/alter predictions
Solve problems
Keep working

after reading

Reflect and contemplate
Reread to refine meaning
Retell, question, discuss
Apply
Read further

As our understanding of reading has deepened, we have recognized that traditional instruction has not supported reading as a strategic, cognitive process. Too often in school, teachers have said to students "Read this book [article, chapter, etc.] for Friday," providing no other guidance until a discussion, quiz, report, or worksheet "finishes" the assignment later on. But such instruction, we now realize, utterly fails to *show* children how to read, to somehow break the task up into its component steps or tasks, and to provide kids with specific strategies they can use to get ready, to construct meaning, and to apply what they've read.

Today, more and more teachers are teaching reading as a process, giving children lots of experiences that invite a strategic approach to comprehension. Literature circles are one manifestation of this trend. The role sheets help students activate their prior knowledge, make predictions, and set purposes *before reading* each selection. The various discussion roles encourage different cognitive approaches to meaning making: visualization (the illustrator), associative thinking (the connector), analysis (the discussion director and vocabulary enricher), drama/performance (the literary luminary).

The actual literature circle group meetings provide rich support to students *during the reading process.* Since students meet regularly *while* they are working through a book, the group meeting supports kids in constructing and comparing interpretations of the book, sharing visualizations, correcting misunderstandings, making connections and predictions, sustaining energy, and keeping the work going. *After reading,* the literature circles model includes varied opportunities for students to reread, rethink, and synthesize what they have learned. There are chances to work both alone and in a group to culminate the reading, and to share the results of one's thinking with a wider community.

Reader Response Literary Criticism

One of the most inspiring stories in American education is that of Louise Rosenblatt, who had a great idea in 1938 and stuck with it. Rosenblatt, of course, is the developer of the "reader response" school of literary criticism. It was her fundamental insight in *Literature as Exploration* that a text is just ink on a page until a reader comes along and gives it life. Debunking the old school of the so-called New Critics, she insisted that there is no one correct interpretation of a literary work, but multiple interpretations, each of them profoundly dependent on the prior experience brought to the text by each reader. Rosenblatt clung to, elucidated, and reexplained this simple, powerful idea for more than fifty years, until it finally began winning widening acceptance in the 1980s.

In recent years, Robert Probst of Georgia State University has emerged as a helpful interpreter of Rosenblatt's ideas for K–12 teachers. In his book *Response and Analysis* (1988), Probst lays out a concise description of reader response theory, applying it to the real situation in public schools. He explains how American teachers, in their hunger to push students up the cognitive ladder to the *analysis* of literature, forget or refuse to begin with students' *response* to their reading. Probst explains that in good teaching, the response always comes first. As he reminds us:

> The pleasures that drew us first to literature were not those of the literary scholar. When our parents read us *Mother Goose,* we enjoyed the rhythms of the language without analyzing the political or social significance of nursery rhymes. Later, we listened to "Little Red Riding Hood," not to identify characteristics of the fairy tale, but to find out whether or not the wolf had the little girl for dinner. And still later, we read *Catcher in the Rye,* not to investigate Salinger's style and trace the literary influences of his book, but to see how Holden Caulfield copes. (p. 3)

In other words, the pathway to analysis, to more sophisticated and defensible interpretations of literature, must go through personal response, not around it. While Probst and Rosenblatt both agree that there are better and worse readings of texts, there are not "wrong" ones. Any work of literature is always a confrontation, a collaboration, between a reader's prior experience and the words of an author.

Literature circles are classroom structures that inherently welcome, celebrate, and build upon students' responses to what they read. Indeed, one inherent safeguard protecting kids' reader response is that the teacher cannot be in every group at once; it's impossible for a backsliding teacher to force premature analysis on more than one student group at a time. Of course, literature circles don't only protect kids' opportunity to respond to literature. They also have within them a variety of incentives and invitations to go beyond response toward evaluation, analysis, and critique.

Independent Reading

As this book is written, in 1994, a great many American elementary schools already have a daily occurrence called SSR (sustained silent reading), or DEAR (drop everything and read), or some other fifteen- or twenty-minute period when everyone in the building—sometimes including cooks and janitors—"just reads." There is no assigned reading in SSR, no quizzes, no strategy lessons, no grading, no book reports, and little or no record keeping. It is simply an official, scheduled acknowledgment of the research showing that reading achievement is more highly correlated with independent reading than with any other single factor. As the landmark study *Becoming a Nation of Readers* (Anderson et al. 1985) states:

> Children should spend more time in independent reading. Independent reading, whether in school or out of school, is associated with gains in reading achievement. By the time they are in third or fourth grade, children should read independently a minimum of two hours per week. Children's reading should include classic and modern works of fiction and nonfiction that represent the core of our cultural heritage. (p. 119)

Of course, the value of independent reading wasn't exactly a hot news flash when the Commission on Reading endorsed it. Twenty years earlier, around the time I started teaching high school, "hooked on books" became an educational phenomenon. Daniel Fader, a former high school teacher and professor at the University of Michigan, came up with a simple idea for energizing secondary reading programs: jettison the thick anthologies and fill the classroom with lots of single copies of novels, especially current adolescent literature. Then, he said, use class time to let kids read and talk about books.

Though Fader's plan lacked the elaborated roles and structures of modern literature circles (or reading workshops), it worked. "Hooked on books" became a movement. All around the country, eager young teachers started scrounging school bookrooms, garage sales, and used-book shops, carrying armloads of books to school. We built our libraries and kids started reading more real books. While Fader's furor eventually faded, he legitimized classroom libraries and independent reading—lasting gifts to the profession. For many young teachers, Fader's book sparked our first classroom libraries and made independent reading a permanent part of our teaching repertoire.

More recently, Richard Anderson (Anderson, Wilson, and Fielding 1988), Richard Allington (1983), and David Pearson (Fielding and Pearson 1994) have reported a number of studies linking independent reading to heightened comprehension and overall reading achievement. Kids need more time to read in school and need to be able to choose their own materials and talk with fellow readers (Fielding and Pearson, p. 64). This kind of time—time to "just read"—has been largely absent from most skill-and-worksheet-driven classrooms. These reading researchers also agree that independent reading time needs to be well structured, that teachers should help students pick books at their fluency level, and that when activities shift to teacher-guided instruction, the focus should be on demonstrations of comprehension strategies rather than so-called subskills. Literature circles are one orderly and manageable structure for ensuring that this kind of substantial independent reading—well beyond the levels customarily supported by SSR programs—happens in school.

Scaffolding Theory

The term "scaffolding" was introduced in the 1950s by cognitive psychologist Jerome Bruner (1961) to describe a special kind of helping that parents give their small children who are learning to speak. The word is a metaphor for the temporary support structures that mothers and fathers instinctively provide as their kids explore language. The classic example of at-home scaffolding is the bedtime story or read-aloud, during which parents intuitively use the "lap method" to teach their children about language, print, or books. The underlying ingredients of this special kind of unconscious teaching interaction are:

Predictability: There is a regular schedule of activities and a regular, recurrent pattern of steps within each event.

Playfulness: Parents and children are open to fun, spontaneity, and feeling. The activities are done primarily for enjoyment and closeness, not for practical outcomes.

Focus on meaning: Language is used to construct meaning and share real ideas. Form takes a back seat to content. Particular language features or ideas may be learned, but they are addressed only when children attempt to use them in real talk, reading, or writing.

Role reversal: Children get many chances to lead—to choose topics or books, to decide when to digress or talk, to elect whether to continue, stop, change topics or books, etc.

Modeling: The parent is a "joyfully literate adult," providing demonstrations of mature and enthusiastic language behavior.

Nomenclature: As scaffolded interaction becomes a regular event, child and parent start developing their own minilanguage for talking about their activities. With bedtime stories, for example, this jargon might include terms like book, story, author, character, picture, ending, cover, and the like.

Though the concept of scaffolding was originally developed to help explain the miracle of young children's oral language acquisition, we now see its generalizability to learning at all ages. After all, if the "lap method" can teach the most complex lesson that any human being ever learns—the thousands of abstract, unconscious rules that constitute any human language—then it is clearly the world's greatest teaching method.

And indeed, the best of today's holistic, integrated classroom activities—strategies like literature circles—owe a huge debt to the insights of Jerome Bruner and the idea of scaffolding. If you look beneath the surface of literature circles, you see teachers scaffolding students' learning. Literature circles are predictable, playful, and meaning-centered activities in which kids exercise lots of choice and responsibility, teachers demonstrate their own literacy, structures are provided that help students function at a higher level than they could unaided, and everyone gradually adopts a new language for talking about their work together: author, character, chapter, genre, problem, conflict, novel, role sheet, discussion group, response log, not to mention discussion director, illustrator, literary luminary, vocabulary enricher, connector, and so forth.

Collaborative Learning

The ten-year-old collaborative/cooperative learning movement is so well established in American schools that it requires no introduction here. There are ample and useful resources for teachers to read and learn about the underlying theory, the key classroom practices, and (for those who need "proof" in terms of the customary measures of educational "success") the huge body of research documenting achievement gains across the curriculum (Johnson, Johnson, Holubec, and Roy 1991). Literature circles are a part—a quite sophisticated and highly evolved part—of the wider collaborative learning movement.

As most professionally active teachers are well aware, the epicenter of the collaborative movement is Minnesota, where brothers David and Roger Johnson, along with a host of colleagues, have developed a wide array of cooperative learning resources. While there are many other cooperative learning experts, authors, agencies, consultants, and workshops around, the Johnson group is always worth listening to because in their work they generally cling to the true, student-empowering potential of genuine collaborative structures. Unlike other popularizers who harness the energizing social processes of small groups to the memorization of the same old pointless trivia—constructs like Robert Slavin's (1985) "team games tournament"—the Johnsons generally apply cooperation to higher-order thinking about worthwhile topics.

As noted earlier, the widespread corruptions and misapplications of cooperative learning have given rise to a growing professional polarization. Today, the term "cooperative learning" is increasingly coming to denote skills-oriented, break-it-down, traditional school tasks assigned by teachers to student groups, while "collaborative learning" is the term preferred by teachers who are trying to sponsor true inquiry in small-group work by designing high-order, student-centered, open-ended activities. Obviously, all the teachers who contributed to this book feel that our kid-run discussion groups represent authentic collaboration. Varied as they are, all of our literature circles display the characteristic features of true collaboration: student-initiated inquiry, choice, self-direction, mutual interdependence, face-to-face interaction, and self- and group assessment.

Still, some of our colleagues would disagree. They are especially troubled by the use of such devices as role sheets to guide students' reading and discussion. They argue that such transitional or helping devices really turn the activity into a convergent, teacher-controlled task. They insist that you cannot "ease into" genuine collaboration or break literature response into pieces. You must plunge into the whole complexity of open-ended discussion the first time you try it with students, or you're breaking learning down in a behavioristic and mechanistic fashion. If this critique fits the version of literature circles described in this book, then our activity would be consigned to the newly downgraded category, cooperative, versus the more exalted designation, collaborative. In one sense, these terminology issues are of little importance—what matters is whether kids read, think, and talk. But, for the record, we will take a minute here to explain why we feel like real collaborationists.

Yes, we do use our discussion role sheets as a temporary, transitional helping tool. We use this tool because our student groups become independent more fully and more quickly than when we don't. We've learned that for kids to start running their own book discussions without teacher intervention or direction, they must have plenty to say—they need to bring lots of their own original ideas and reactions to the group. How do we make sure this happens? We offer temporary support devices that help kids to "harvest" their own responses, ideas, and questions during reading—and bring them along. Then, after a brief period, the kids gather their own. We think that our roles provide a kind of surrogate adult help in the child's zone of proximal development: as Vygotsky (1978) says, what children can do with our help today, they can do on their own tomorrow.

We designed our own set of discussion roles so that each embodies one fundamental way that readers think—visualizing, connecting, associating, analyzing, reading aloud, and so forth. For kids who are not yet fluent at surfacing their own deep and diverse reader responses, the role sheets invite and capture those reactions. The roles help kids flex and limber up some different ways of responding to a text, ways they already possess. In this sense—and in this sense only—our discussion roles do temporarily "break down" reading into parts. However, this is never more than a fraction of the picture. When the groups meet, the main goal is always to have a natural conversation about the book, which means that all kinds of responses and topics are welcome from all group members at all meetings. The daily discussion role is only one element of what each kid brings to the group, something the group can refer to if they need to or want to as the conversation unfolds.

Still in all, we certainly agree that these small-group "tools" are a very tricky structure, always susceptible to stealing kids' ownership of the very activity they're designed to unloose. That's why we're careful about the kind of roles we use, how we use them, and for how long. In the same spirit, we join our "purist" colleagues in rejecting "empty" group roles—nonsubstantive, nonthinking tasks like recorder, secretary, process checker, and so forth. These very commonly adopted cooperative learning group jobs, we would agree, often fragment learning without enhancing students' ownership of the process or their understanding of ideas. Such content-free roles divide up work in student groups and divide up meaning as well. Such roles usually don't enhance thinking, invite autonomy, or create sustained, natural conversations about anything.

Group Dynamics

In my own previous work with Steven Zemelman (Daniels and Zemelman 1985; Zemelman and Daniels 1988), he and I have tried to import the insights of group dynamics into discussions of instruction and school reform. We think it's odd that the rather well developed and extensive field called group dynamics is neglected by school teachers, people whose very livelihoods depend upon orchestrating complex, extended group experiences. Obviously, the popularizers of collaborative learning have drawn many of their structures and procedures from the literature of group dynamics, though the connections are rarely explicit and acknowledged. Pioneers like Carl Rogers (1969), Herbert Thelen (1954), Richard and Patricia Schmuck (1988), Louis Thayer (1981), and their colleagues are rarely mentioned when the basic designs for small-group activities—which these people pioneered—are described.

The overarching insight of group dynamics is that there are certain *predictable and controllable elements* in the development of mature, productive, interdependent groups. Since any school classroom—and any subgroup within it—is subject to these dynamics, it is vital for teachers to understand and "steer" these elements. This is exactly what Zemelman and I tried to explain in an essay called "What Every Teacher Should Know About Group Dynamics," which appears in our book *A Community of Writers* (1988). I won't attempt to rewrite that chapter here, but I will summarize one set of key principles that helps explain why literature circles are such a powerful group structure.

Group dynamics research tells us that there are six ingredients that must be nurtured in the development of any mature, interdependent, productive group (Schmuck and Schmuck 1988):

- Clear expectations.
- Mutually developed norms.
- Shared leadership and responsibility.
- Open channels of communication.
- Diverse friendship patterns.
- Conflict resolution mechanisms.

In classroom literature circles, each of these factors is explicitly provided for in the training, development, and maintenance of the discussion groups. Indeed, the very *essence* of literature circles involves predictable structures and events; clear, student-made procedures; kid leadership and responsibility; classwide friendships; constant public and private talk and writing among everyone in the room; and *inviting* disagreements and conflicting interpretations to emerge within a safe and comfortable structure.

In other words, from a group dynamics point of view, literature circles are a very well-structured activity, one that we would expect not only to be successful in accomplishing its task goal—which is the clear and deep understanding of a book—but also to contribute to the general cohesiveness and productivity of the wider classroom community.

Detracking

One of the reasons literature circles have coalesced so strongly and generated so much excitement among teachers is that *they make heterogeneous classrooms work*. You can have a very diverse class of kids, with widely mixed "ability" levels, assorted cultural and ethnic identities, even lots of mainstreamed special education children, and still have an exciting, challenging, orderly, and caring atmosphere for everyone. In other words, literature circles—along with reading and writing workshops—are a key structure for detracking schools, which is one of the greatest unsolved issues of educational justice in our country.

Researchers like Jeannie Oakes (1985), Anne Wheelock (1992), and George Wood (1992) have voluminously documented the fact that ability grouping in American schools harms the achievement of kids in low and middle groups while providing few if any benefits for the kids in top groups. Further, Richard Allington (1983) has shown that the quality of instruction in low-track reading groups is consistently poorer than that offered to kids ranked as "higher" readers. There is simply no educational justification—and there is great social harm—in segregating kids into "Bluebirds," "Chickadees," and "Buzzards" groups, based on tested or perceived ability levels.

However, given that teachers and parents alike are deeply influenced by the "normal" ability-grouped model of instruction, how can we escape this destructive tradition? Literature circles are a natural substitution. Kids can still read at their own level, but they now do so by grouping *themselves*—not as externally labeled "Buzzards" but as people who are choosing one book at a time. Because the class includes students who are reading at all levels, a student can spend some time with skilled, above-grade-level readers—people who model the next step up—and at other times can "take a break," reading at his or her own comfort level with some other friends. The different discussion roles used in groups invite different learning styles to shine—kids who may not offer glib plot summaries can offer moving read-alouds or unique illustrations. Indeed, effective reading discussion groups tend to see diversity as an asset—the more people talk about books, the more they want to have a *range* of responses, ideas, and connections in the group. It's not as much fun if everyone has the same experiences, stories, connections to share; discussions are richer if people *aren't* all alike.

In a literature circles classroom, there are so many ways to succeed, to find your niche as a reader. The teacher, of course, plays an important role, kidwatching with care, balancing between challenging each child and sustaining, above all, the love of reading, writing, and talking about books. And, of course, because the role of presenter/taskmaster of round-robin reading has been renounced, the teacher is now *available* to take a facilitative role and if kids are struggling, to give individual attention while the rest of the students work along in their kid-led groups.

Balancing Instruction

Steve Zemelman and I sometimes joke that if we ever get run over by a bus, we hope someone will write on our tombstones that we at least promoted balance in reading-writing instruction. We are concerned that in most schools, most kids' literacy experiences are unbalanced in a variety of ways. We believe—and much recent research powerfully confirms—that kids need three vital kinds of balance:

- Balance between teacher-guided and self-directed reading.
- Balance between wide and close (what Peterson and Eeds [1990] call "extensive" and "intensive") reading.
- Balance in the kind of social interaction they experience around books.

We can represent these kinds of balance on three parallel continuums:

Student-Directed		Teacher-Directed

Individual	Small Group	Whole Class

Extensive		Intensive
(fast, quick reading; focus on enjoyment and quantity)		(careful, deep reading; focus on author's craft and literary elements)

We can now use this device to illustrate the problem of balance by laying out some of the most widely used classroom structures for teaching reading. Obviously, the "accurate" location for any real classroom activity depends mightily on the teacher and kids who use it. Most of these structures can be shaded quite far in any direction—after all, some teachers give quizzes in SSR and others conduct genuinely nondirective whole-group discussions. But still, if we envision the usual manifestation of each model, we'll get a sense of how they sort out.

SSR RW LC		PE GR RR
Student-Directed		Teacher-Directed

SSR RW	RR PE LC	GR
Individual	Small Group	Whole Class

SSR RW	LC	GR TR PE
Extensive		Intensive

RR = Traditional three-group round-robin reading

GR = Guided reading; lecture/discussion method (typical secondary school English class or elementary whole-class lesson)

SSR = Sustained silent reading

RW = Reading workshop (Nancie Atwell model)

LC = Literature circles (this book's model)

PE = Literature study groups (Peterson and Eeds model)

Perhaps this illustration helps point up the important role our version of literature circles can play in a balanced reading program. They are the only structure that combines the elements of student-directed, small-group, moderately intensive reading. Most of the other small-group models currently used in school are highly teacher controlled, as are many newer models featured in the professional literature. For example, the "literature studies" models of Peterson and Eeds (1990), Samway et al. (1991), and many others frequently featured in teacher magazines combine small-group social processes with intensive reading and a high degree of teacher direction—which of course, often comes along with detailed study of literary elements.

There's not a "right side" to this chart. It's not meant to raise one structure above another, but to help us all build balance into the days, weeks, and years we design for kids. However, while there is no correct side, if you are running a classroom in which all the reading activities fall on the right-hand side of this chart (or the left-hand side), then your program may be unbalanced. If you are doing nothing but reading workshop, SSR, and literature circles, you may want to rebalance by adding an element of intensive reading, making sure kids linger longer and more thoughtfully over some texts. If you are doing lots of whole-class guided reading lessons and also doing Peterson/Eeds–style literature studies in small groups, then you might want to add an element of student direction to the mix, starting up some literature circles or initiating a reading workshop. If you believe, as we do, in balance, then the goal is not to be right but to offer our students a rich diversity of reading experiences.

Literature Circles Ancestors

As I said at the beginning of this chapter, many of the ideas behind literature circles, though old, can be traced to specific people, pioneers (sometimes lonely ones) in their fields. Some of these—Louise Rosenblatt, Kathy Short, Jerry Harste, the Johnsons, Kurt Lewin, and others—have already been acknowledged. But there are other ancestors of literature circles whose contributions are perhaps more indirect and yet just as essential. They have given us the foundation upon which we're building a whole new segment of the school day. If literature circles "stick" this time around and become a permanent part of the regular school schedule in America, there will be a new bright spot in every day for millions of kids and teachers. So, let us take a minute to thank:

John Dewey

Whenever progressive, student-centered school reforms emerge, John Dewey is always somewhere in the background. I trust he's smiling down at our literature circles. Every important idea underlying literature circles, Dewey explained at length three generations ago, in *Democracy and Education* (1916) and his many other works. Literature circles embody Dewey's tenets of learning by doing, of creating a real learning-living community, of kids taking responsibility and making choices, of teachers serving as guides and coaches—and above all, his conception of children as fundamentally good, self-regulating, growth-seeking creatures who need to be empowered, not controlled.

Carl Rogers

Rogers was the father of humanistic education, and literature circles are a true manifestation of his philosophy, featuring student ownership, involvement, and choice. Back in the 1960s, Rogers scandalized the educational establishment with his infamous statement that anything you could *teach* anyone was by definition either trivial or harmful. Instead of teaching, Rogers promoted *facilitation,* the process by which the leader takes a step back and is satisfied (indeed honored) to take the role of scene setter, helper, partner, and coach instead of the ego-feeding but limiting role of expert authority. In the literature circles classroom, genuine and subtle facilitation skills are the teacher's main contribution. Rogers understood that learners do the learning, and his insights have been—and will continue to be—a strong undercurrent in the thinking of all progressive educators.

James Moffett

Moffett is one of the most important and yet relatively unsung leaders of literacy education over the past twenty-five years, and the title of his major work speaks of his contribution eloquently: *Student Centered Language Arts K–12* (Moffett and Wagner 1992). In a half-dozen books and countless workshops, Moffett has steadily and eloquently preached the importance of kids' choosing and doing their own reading, writing, speaking, and listening—with a stress on playfulness, delight, exploration, and community. His commercially published (and before-its-time) integrated language arts program called *Interaction* included literature discussion activities very much like today's literature circles. Moffett has also been a strong champion of real literature in school programs, and has written sensitively about the public fears and censorship efforts that such teaching can inspire.

Neil Postman

In their classic 1967 school reform time bomb, *Teaching as a Subversive Activity,* Postman and colleague Charles Weingartner challenged us hyperdirective schoolteachers to limit ourselves to three questions a day. When I tried this experiment in my Chicago vocational high school classroom, the three-question quota lasted about three minutes. The first one was "We're gonna try something new today you guys, okay?" My freshmen cracked this code immediately and gleefully called me on every inadvertent question. ("Is Touché here today?" was number two, as I recall.) What I learned from this experiment—and from Postman and Weingartner's eloquent critique—was that in genuinely educational classrooms, the questions should come *from the students.* Well-run literature circles take that dictum very seriously. In his much maligned follow-up, *Teaching as a Conserving Activity* (1979), Postman added another enduring idea to the literature of educational reform. Schools, he argued, should have a *thermostatic* function in relation to society. That is, if the general culture is awash in television, media, and visual images, then schools should not cater but counter. Instead of competing to be more media-wise, school should be otherwise, by offering students the most attractive and involving possible immersion in another world—*the world of the book.* Again, literature circles take Postman's prescriptions—both those of the radical sixties and the thoughtful seventies—very much to heart.

Recent Research on Literature Circles: Does It Work?

The body of research on literature groups is growing quickly. Unfortunately, these studies appear under so many different names (literature studies, literature discussion groups, book clubs, literature circles, cooperative book discussion groups) and often combine so many divergent ingredients (teacher control versus student autonomy, assigned versus chosen books) that one has to read very carefully. All kinds of evidence, support, and teacher testimonials are accumulating about literature circles—if you know what each researcher means by literature circles.

Probably one of the most helpful and important volumes currently available is Kathy Short and Kathryn Mitchell Pierce's *Talking About Books* (1990), which presents the reports of a dozen teacher-researchers who have implemented a variety of literature group approaches. Each of these veteran whole language teachers is deeply committed to the value of literature and to honoring kids' voices, so each of the fascinating variations described there deserves a respectful hearing.

There have been many encouraging articles by teacher-practitioners in recent journals. Suzi Keegan and Karen Shrake reported in the April 1991 *Reading Teacher* of their success with fourth-grade literature study groups in a Maryland school. Keegan and Shrake's account is particularly noteworthy because their group discussion model was explicitly designed as an alternative to ability grouping. Katherine Samway and five colleagues from the Oakland, California, area offered their model of "literature study circles" in the November 1991 *Reading Teacher*. In several very diverse, multilingual, fifth- and sixth-grade classrooms, literature groups were linked to several valued outcomes: (1) kids understood themselves and others better, (2) they saw themselves as readers, (3) they became aware of different approaches to reading instruction, and (4) they expressed a strong preference for activities with more choice and student control. Working with older students and reporting in the *English Journal* (September 1992), Elizabeth Egan Close shared a model of literature groups that helped high school students think more deeply about literature, gain confidence in their own ideas, and work out puzzlements and confusions together. Her model features a quite elaborate training sequence for students, leading them into the group work one step at a time, and also retains a central, reciprocal role for whole-group discussion. All three of the above classroom studies include a very high measure of teacher-directedness, and (using the terms of one of our earlier continuums) they all focus mainly on intensive rather than extensive reading. Therefore, they are not validations of this book's model, but rather are reports of our cousins' successes, stories of progress within the family.

For those who are interested in whether literature circles can raise test scores, it is a bit too early. Probably because the activity and the terminology are relatively new, few researchers have yet correlated participation in literature circles with achievement on standardized tests. One important exception was reported in the January 1993 *English Journal.* Martin Nystrand and his colleagues at the University of Wisconsin initially studied 217 episodes of cooperative grouping in high school literature classes—activities that sounded a lot like literature circles. In order to assess the effectiveness of this strategy, the researchers devised a year-end, all-essay test of literature learning, which included three kinds of items:

1. Did kids remember some of what they had read (could they retell basic plots or identify characters in novels)?
2. Could they talk about some of the themes or "big ideas" they discovered in the books?
3. Could they discuss and reflect intelligently upon their own personal response to the book in question?

It seemed a fair test.

Comparing the results on this test between kids in cooperative group classes and traditional teacher-centered programs, Nystrand was surprised to find that the *students in literature discussion groups actually scored lower* than students in teacher-directed programs. Given the voluminous positive research on cooperative learning structures in so many other subject areas, the researchers were suspicious. So Nystrand and his colleagues decided to take another look. In restudying classrooms self-defined by their teachers as collaborative, the researchers found that 89 percent of these classrooms in fact were not cooperative at all. Instead, these teachers had typically instituted what Nystrand calls "collaborative seatwork." What these informants were calling collaboration, in essence, were activities in which they instructed students: "Here are ten factual recall questions about the chapter you read for today. Look up the answers together and hand them in by 2:10." While teachers might label such activities "collaborative," they were exactly the same kind of right-answer literature instruction that literature circles were designed to avoid.

In the following year Nystrand's group looked at another group of classrooms, carefully controlling for the genuineness of the student-centered discussion groups. Under these new standards, the students participating in genuine literature-circle-like activity scored *twice as far above the test mean as the previous year's "fake" circle groups had fallen beneath it.* The moral of this story is: literature circles work well when they are done correctly. When the name is simply applied to the traditional, teacher-dominated, factual-recall activities, no advantage is gained.

The key ingredients in effective, genuinely collaborative small reading-group discussions, Nystrand found, were:

- That the group activities were well structured.
- That groups had genuine autonomy and responsibility.
- That discussion tasks or prompts were open-ended.
- That the students' main job was to construct new knowledge together and to build meaning and interpretations, not to reach predetermined conclusions or results.

These, of course, are exactly the conditions that skillful literature circle teachers are trying to create when they set up groups, establish procedures, train their kids, and turn them loose to read and talk about books.

CHAPTER THREE

• • • • • • • • •

*Getting Started: Preparing
and Orienting Students*

Literature circles are really fun! Lit circles are very neat. They are very, very awesome. Lit circles are very, very complicated, through.
    —Stacey, fifth grade

These kids are amazing! They really work at pulling everyone into the discussion, they're kind and thoughtful . . . I never have to get them back on task, they're so involved in what they're doing. . . . It just blows my mind that they can do so much when you just guide them and let them go.
    —Kristen Overcash, fifth-grade teacher

THESE TWO statements quite nicely embody the realities of preparing students to do literature circles. Getting a basic version going is usually relatively simple because the structure is self-teaching. However, literature circles *are* inarguably complex, including as they do a decentralized classroom, lots of different books being read, multiple rotating roles being played, lots of logs and role sheets circulating, the frequent reshuffling of groups, plenty of noise and movement, and a wide range of choices for the teacher. This means that while you can easily jump start some "rough draft" literature circles, the longer-term process of fine-tuning and problem solving will take time, patience, creativity, artifice, and stick-to-itiveness. But it's worth it.

Chapters 6 and 7 offer detailed stories of how fifteen different teachers started and are now running their own versions of lit circles. Their classes

50

range from kindergarten to primary special education to the intermediate grades to junior high to Chapter I to high school honors to a college criminology course—so there's a model there for everyone. But good ideas aren't tied to the grade level at which they originated: lots of the best innovations are completely translatable to other grade levels. For example, Debbie Gurvitz has third graders teach literature circles to her kindergartners—there's no reason why older kids of any age can't teach lit circles to younger ones, or vice versa.

Since these classroom veterans have so many variations to share later on, this chapter will simply offer two general versions of literature circle training that have served well in a variety of contexts: a quick and a careful version. But first, a brief note on the word "training." In some quarters, training is a politically incorrect term: it labels you as a Skinnerian behaviorist bent on dehumanizing children and atomizing the curriculum. Unfortunately, the English language has not yet supplied us with an alternative word that substitutes semantically for "an organized procedure for preparing a group of people for some experience." Therefore, over the next few pages, we use the term "training" as shorthand for a quite humanistic, sensitive, and respectful way of getting kids ready to run their own literature circles.

Two Versions of Training

Some students and classes seem to need more step-by-step preparation than others to function effectively in literature circles. They just don't get the gestalt of this complex activity right away. In fact, even in the classrooms of very progressive teachers, kids may already be so socialized to right answers and so dependent on outside authority that they are reluctant to plunge in. This can happen even in the primary grades, where children haven't yet spent much time being brainwashed by basals and worksheets. Many of the teachers who report success with lit circles say they have used a quite careful, staged training period. That's the careful version we'll talk about in a minute.

Other students and classes, who've had lots of prior experience with true reader response activities and cooperative group structures, can learn literature circles much more quickly. Often one class period is enough to give a basic overview, introduce one set of role sheets, and have the students practice on a poem or short article. Marline Pearson, the criminology professor for the college course mentioned above, takes just one and a half class sessions to teach her students lit circles—but of course, during that preparation time they are reading and discussing criminology material, so the time isn't "wasted." When you realize that these students have been in school for at least thirteen years without yet learning how to work effectively in cooperative small-group structures, the time certainly seems well worth it.

Quick Training

With warmed-up, collaboration-wise students—or kids already accustomed to a literature-based whole language classroom—an hour is about all it takes to introduce literature circles. One simple way is described below. (If you want to shorten the reading time and still retain a full demonstration, students can read poems, articles, short stories, or picture books instead of chunks of whole books. You may also elect to have everyone read the same story; then the trade-off is between being able to compare notes across the whole class and no longer having the element of student choice. It's a toss-up.)

1. Provide a wide choice of good books, and invite everyone to "choose themselves into" a group of four people that want to read the same book. This will take a few minutes of informal negotiation.
2. Hand out sets of role sheets and let people in each group divvy them up however they want (it's fun to watch art-phobic older kids try to get rid of the illustrator role, which of course is primary kids' favorite).
3. Have someone serving in each role read aloud its description for the whole class, so that everyone hears what other roles will be part of the group. At this point, you can clarify the nature of each role and answer any questions.
4. Give a set amount of time for reading and role-sheet preparation (twenty to thirty minutes is plenty; you'll need less if you're using poems, obviously). Tell the groups to assign themselves a section of the book that everyone feels can comfortably be finished in *five minutes less than* the allotted time. The remaining five minutes will be used to prepare the role sheet (this can be done either during or after reading, but there needs to be time for stopping to write).
5. When everyone has done the reading and prepared the sheets, invite

groups to get together for fifteen or twenty minutes. Clearly explain that the main goal is to have *a natural conversation about the book.* Encourage each role player to "chip in" as the conversation unfolds. Everyone should look for a spontaneous opening. The discussion director is supposed to moderate, keep an eye on the clock, and invite members who haven't joined in to share their ideas.

6. During the conversations, visit each group unobtrusively for a few minutes, strictly as an observer. Be sure not to "steer" the discussion! Jot down specific examples and comments to make during the debriefing.

7. Call the class together for a debriefing in which everyone discusses problems, brainstorms solutions, and shares successes. Have students switch roles and read another section for next time. (This isn't *training* anymore—now they're *doing* literature circles.)

That's it, although you should continue to hold debriefing sessions regularly to make sure everyone's on board.

Careful Training

To find a model for slower, more thorough training in literature circles, we could do no better than follow Barbara Dress into a classroom. Barbara is a former teacher and reading consultant for Palatine School District 15. She recently took early retirement so that she could consult on lit circles with teachers in Chicago and suburban schools. With Sandy King's third graders at Marion Jordan School, Barbara worked for two weeks, about forty-five minutes a day. Sandy's kids were in great shape to start literature circles—their reading and language arts program is rich and literature based. Sandy reads aloud to her students daily, the kids have an active writing workshop, and they think of themselves as real authors. With Sandy and me observing and occasionally helping, here's what Barbara did, first in a quick overview and then in detail.

Overview

Day 1
- kids read a good story and discuss it; the idea of literature circles is introduced

Days 2–5

- kids learn *one role per day* using short stories
- groups of four students *in the same role* meet daily to discuss
- whole class meets to *debrief and clarify* the day's target role

Days 6–10

- kids put the roles together while reading a short novel
- groups of four students in *different roles* meet to discuss; roles rotate daily
- whole class meets daily to *debrief and share*

Step by Step

Day 1: Barbara greets the kids, who are wearing nametags so that she can quickly learn their names. Graciously, she asks if anyone has ever heard of literature circles. No one has any actual experience, but this doesn't stop third graders from speculating on the definition. Barbara welcomes everything and jots key words on the overhead. She then incorporates kids' ideas and language into an overview of the activity.

She tells the kids that they will be working for two weeks on this project, taking one step at a time. She also tells them they will be reading several great stories this week and a good book next week. The rest of this session is given over to the story "The Flying Patchwork Quilt," by Barbara Brenner. Barbara reads the story out loud, slowly and dramatically, stopping a couple of times to invite kids' predictions and clarifications. When she's done, she invites students' comments and responses, and a lively whole-class discussion ensues. Barbara has done her job for this day, which was simply to get acquainted, build some trust, share a good story, and model for the kids the delight of rich discussion topics.

Day 2: Today, Barbara wants to help kids learn the role of *discussion director* as she's adapted it especially for this class. Before handing out that role sheet, she talks to kids about open-ended questions. Referring to the story from yesterday, she asks kids to remember or think of some possible questions about the story. As kids offer suggestions, Barbara makes a distinction between "fat" and "skinny" questions. Skinny ones can be answered in a word or two, she explains, leaving nothing more to say. "Fat" questions on the other hand, you can say lots and lots about. There aren't necessarily right answers to these questions, Barbara says, and everyone can have different things to say about a *really* fat question.

Now she hands out copies of the discussion director role sheet and another short story. She invites kids to read the story, think of two or three really "fat" questions about it, and jot them on their role sheet. This time, kids can read the story several different ways. Ms. King is reading it aloud in one corner, so those who want (or need) to have the story read to them can go there. Alternately, groups can pick one of their own members to read it to the others, and one group elects this option. Other kids read silently. A couple of partners sit on the floor reading alternate pages to each other. As kids begin to finish, Barbara reminds them to jot some fat questions on their DD sheets.

Next, kids go into their groups and meet for ten minutes or so, sharing and discussing their fat questions. Barbara, Sandy, and I circulate, available to help, but not really needed. The kids have plenty to say. For the last few minutes, we gather as a whole group again and Barbara takes sample questions from each group. As always, she skillfully praises and shapes, making sure kids understand what kinds of questions a good discussion director brings to a group.

Day 3: Today, Barbara teaches kids the role of *passage master.* Using a third story, she follows the same pattern as yesterday, first explaining the basic idea of the role and then helping kids brainstorm good examples. One important skill for passage masters (and word wizards, coming up tomorrow) is being able to locate things quickly in the text, so Barbara spends a good deal of time showing kids how to mark on their sheet the page and paragraph of passages they want to share.

Now, the kids read a story as passage masters. When they're done, they meet in their same homogeneous, four-member groups to try out the role. There's plenty of noise, of course, as kids read aloud their favorite sections. When they finish meeting, volunteers from different groups share examples of what passages they picked and tell why. There is further discussion about the problem of locating your passages. Tomorrow's session will provide more practice on this. Again, Barbara gently and subtly shapes kids' responses, reinforcing contributions that genuinely fulfill the passage master role.

Day 4: Today, Barbara teaches kids the role of *word wizard.* She follows the same pattern, first explaining the role, then helping kids practice it by thinking of noteworthy words from yesterday's story. Finally, she sets them to reading another new story with the WW sheet in hand. The kids then meet in their groups and try out the role. When they finish, Barbara asks volunteers from different groups to share examples of the words they focused on.

Day 5: Today, Barbara teaches kids the fourth (and most popular!) role in this set: the *artful artist* (or illustrator). She talks about responding to the reading with a picture instead of with words, and gets kids talking about the importance of the illustrations in favorite books. She stresses that whatever pictures they chose to draw as illustrators do not have to depict actual events or scenes in the story, but can represent personal thoughts, feelings, or connections—even abstractions or designs. Then she goes over the official artful artist role sheet, gives kids one last story to read, and they go to work. Because of kids' pride and care in their artwork, this role sheet takes a little longer than the others to prepare, and Barbara has to work to get them back to their groups. Gradually, kids return to their groups and take turns sharing their graphic responses to the reading. When they are done, Barbara asks volunteers from different groups to show examples of their illustrations. Barbara asks kids to tell what conversations sprung up around the pictures, so they get the message that the drawings are to extend the discussion, not just for decoration.

Days 6–10: Now it's time to put the literature circles together. So this week Ms. King's third graders will read a whole novel, meeting daily in their groups—the same four-member groups that trained together, role by role, last week. The book, selected by Barbara for its wide appeal, is *The Chocolate Touch* by Melanie Chatoff. A takeoff on the King Midas tale, this is a genuinely funny story about a young boy who suddenly develops. . . . well, the title says it.

Each day's session is divided into two roughly twenty-minute parts: reading time and group meetings. During the reading time, kids are free to read the assigned chapters (about fifteen big-type pages per day), work on their role sheets, or (if they have already finished both, which is rare) read something else. Kids who are slower readers need all the reading time they can get; some are doing part of the reading at home, a few with help from a parent or sibling. All kids have to budget their time so that they will be ready to play their assigned role.

When groups meet, Barbara and Sandy circulate to observe, assist, and help solve problems. Since it is a good, involving book, kids have plenty to say, and the discussions go well. The kids discuss about one-fifth of the book each day, and on Friday, there is a general whole-class conversation when everyone reflects back over the two-week learning process. The kids are pleased and proud of themselves, and a bit sad to say goodbye to this dynamic white-haired lady who has brought such a special treat into their classroom each morning.

Barbara, who is an inveterate educational tinkerer, is already talking about all the things she will change the *next* time she models literature circles in a classroom. She's thinking maybe she should introduce the illustrator role first, since it is the kids' favorite, and it helps the students who aren't fluent writers to enter their group on an equal footing. But for Ms. King's kids, the job is well done. They "get it." They understand the system and—most important—they love it.

Ms. King is impressed, too. As the year goes on, she uses literature circles steadily, as a regular and recurrent part of her classroom schedule. Since the training period is now over, kids pick their own books and move among constantly reforming groups, and much less teacher intervention is needed. A few months later, Sandy looks back and writes: "There is a lot of discussion going on and kids love the freedom they have to choose. The kids are more accountable for what they read, they know what to look for while they read (they monitor their comprehension, so to speak) and they really enjoy it!"

Training Variations and Suggestions

Teachers in our lit circles network have shared a number of other tips about orienting and training students, especially when things don't go smoothly and troubleshooting is needed.

- Have older kids teacher younger ones.
- Have experienced lit circle kids train other kids, regardless of age (younger ones can teach older ones).
- Make a videotape of lit circles in your or someone else's classroom; you can use it to train kids next year. (Colleagues can also borrow the tape.) These tapes work best when the students plan, write, and perform the narrative.
- Have kids *visit* a classroom in which lit circles are working well—a few at a time, of course.

- Use *fishbowl demonstrations* for training and problem solving. Ask one lit circle to hold its discussion in the middle of the room while everyone else observes, perhaps taking notes for later debriefing. If you want to demonstrate a certain problem, or model a helpful strategy, you can "cook" the membership of group. Or, to be absolutely sure, you can become a member of the fishbowl group yourself. A helpful addition is the "freeze" feature—a rule that allows anyone observing the fishbowl to stop the action to ask a participant to explain a comment, suggest another course of action, or make an observation. When the freeze discussion is over, the group continues talking about the book until the next freeze is called. Yes, it sounds artificial, but students in fishbowls usually seem perfectly able to carry on despite the interruptions.

CHAPTER FOUR

Scheduling and Managing Groups

PROBABLY THE number one question teachers have when they start thinking about managing literature circles is, Where in the world am I gonna get all those books? That's why Chapter 5 is devoted entirely to getting books and other lit circle materials into your classroom.

Meanwhile, don't wait. While a huge classroom library is a nice thing to develop over time, you don't *need* one to begin lit circles. You can use a class set of the *same* novel to start things off, ask the librarian to dig up some multiple-copy sets, or rummage through the bookroom. If you keep scrounging, in no time you'll have enough books to keep kids going.

Group Size and Formation

What size groups work best for literature circles? In the ideal classroom, group size would be determined by the number of kids who freely choose a particular book or article. The factor moderating pure choice, of course, is that we want to form *small, functional* discussion groups of people *reading the same stuff* (except for intentionally heterogeneous groups, discussed in Chapter 10). That means teachers must balance offering real choice against massaging kids into groups containing a functional number of members. Among our Chicago-area literature circle teachers, the favorite group size seems to be four or five, at least for kids in the intermediate grades and up. This allows a good variety of roles to be played and perspectives to be offered without the group's getting so big that distractions and inefficiencies take over. This size is also realistic for schools where lots of kids are absent every day, for one reason or another. With at least three remaining members, a circle can go along fine. For younger kids, some teachers like to keep the group size smaller—three or four, perhaps even using pairs in the early primary grades (see Chapter 6 for more details on primary-grade applications).

In practice, many factors force teachers to have groups larger or smaller than the optimal four or five. When six kids want to read the same book, you have to decide whether two groups of three or one group of six will be more productive—balancing active participation against diversity of ideas. When only two kids are interested in a book, the teacher has to ponder whether the pair in question can really feed each other or whether each should move along to a second-choice title that will pull them into a larger group. Obviously, in order to get groups of decent size, teachers will have to do more than massage—they may have to negotiate, cajole, finagle, bargain, logroll, backpat, or bribe. Literature circle teachers are often heard saying things like, OK, if you'll read *Hatchet* now, and be the fourth member of this group, I'll help you get a group together for *The Phantom Tollbooth* next cycle.

In the everyday practice of literature circles, most students in the room *won't* be reading their absolute number-one-choice-in-the-whole-world book—many people will have compromised to make the system work. But we notice in working with kids at all grade levels that even just adding the smallest degree of control—like deciding whether you're going to read a certain book now instead of later, or getting your third choice instead of no choice at all—feels welcome and makes a big difference in motivation. And as teachers get more books in their room, as kids develop more skill with their roles, as the norms of student-centered learning are built and reinforced, more and more true choices become available.

Role Sheets

How They Work

Other than kids and books, the most important ingredient in newly formed literature circles is the set of *role sheets,* which give a different task to each group member—both for the individual reading and for the group discussion. In Chapter 5 are copies of some of the roles teachers have used with success, including some comments on the strengths, peculiarities, and problems of each. The "basic," generic roles that work well for students in about fourth grade through college are listed first, followed by a section of role sheets especially designed for primary kids, and then by a variety of other sheets keyed to particular students or types of reading.

Before we look at the basic roles, a few comments. First of all, as we have already said, the role sheets are supposed to be transitional, temporary devices. *The goal of all role sheets is to make role sheets obsolete.* Secondly, all of these task descriptions are designed to support genuine *collaborative learning* by giving kids clearly defined, interlocking jobs to do. Further, the sheets enact some important ideas about *reading*: among these, that readers who approach a text with their prior knowledge activated and with some clear-cut, conscious *purposes* will comprehend more. So the role sheets are meant to help kids read better *and* discuss better. There is also a management dimension to the role sheets: whenever teachers move to a decentralized cooperative group structure, they are essentially giving up some degree of direct guidance over the kids, and so the role sheets are a kind of teacher surrogate—a written guide to the work at hand.

How do these sheets figure in a real-life lit circle group meeting? They exist to help spark or sustain natural conversation, not to guide or provide the bulk of the talk. This means that when a group sits down to talk, the conversation may be started by anyone, may take off in any direction, and needn't return. There's no obligation to "work through" any or all of the notes on people's role sheets. Indeed, if kids or teachers misconstrue the role sheets as the main focus of a group's interaction, then literature circles can become a kind of oral workbook. Group members may take turns marching mechanically through their roles, reading their notes aloud. There will be no interaction, debate, challenge, give-and-take, no building on other people's ideas and interpretations. Such misdirected groups tend to finish their "discussion" quickly and then stare at each other with nothing left to say.

This is why we often tell students that in a successful lit circle meeting you may never refer to your role sheets. After all, if everyone comes to the group with lots to talk about, who needs a sheet? Especially in the beginning days of lit circles, we make sure that students don't mistake the role sheets for a business-as-usual worksheet in disguise. Since respecting students' ideas and inviting genuine conversation into the classroom is contrary to most kids' experience of schooling, we have to highlight the shift in expectations that literature circles embody.

In mature literature circle classrooms, role sheets are usually aban-doned when groups are capable of lively, text-centered, multifaceted book discussions drawn from open-ended entries in *response logs*. How do groups reach this stage? By using the roles for a good while, repeatedly adopting a half-dozen different angles on their reading; by amassing a repertoire of group discussion roles; and by practicing within a safe structure until less guidance is needed. Once kids have used a variety of roles and had plenty of successful group meetings, then the structured roles are less necessary, and wise teachers phase them out, replacing them with a reading log. After all, the goal of literature circles is to have natural and sophisticated discussions of literature—and once that is happening, we want to remove any artificial or limiting elements immediately.

Selecting a Mix of Roles

Once the range of acceptable group sizes has been determined, teachers need to figure out what roles they wish to use and in what combinations. Here's a priority list we've been using in Chicago with some success (complete role sheets appear on pages 77 to 104):

Required Roles	Optional Roles
Discussion director	Researcher
Literary luminary/passage master	Summarizer/essence extractor
Connector	Character captain
Illustrator	Vocabulary enricher/word master
	Travel tracer/scene setter

We've found it helpful for every group to have a *discussion director,* someone who has official responsibility to think up some good discussion questions, convene the meeting, and solicit contributions from the other members. We also feel that the *literary luminary/passage master* role is always valuable, because this person takes readers back to memorable, important sections of the text and reads them aloud. The *connector* is crucial because this member takes everyone from the text world out into the real world, where readers' experience connects with literature. Finally, we add the *illustrator* to our list of mandatory roles because it invites a graphic, nonlinguistic response to the text—and this role often elicits very helpful contributions from kids who don't always succeed at the usual school-language prompts. These four roles ensure four different "takes" on the text: the discursive/analytical (discussion director), the oral/dramatic (literary luminary), the associative (connector) and the graphic/artistic (illustrator). Using these four roles as a base, the teacher or kids can select roles to fill out the group, depending on the nature of the book and the reading goals at hand. For reading self-selected fiction titles, many of our colleagues have drawn from the optional roles listed above for assigning roles to various-size groups. In a pinch, of course, a large group can have *two* of almost any role, illustrators, connectors—even dual discussion directors can be fine as long as power struggles don't ensue!

I want to reiterate here, as elsewhere, that these roles are meant to *rotate* each time the groups meet, so that as students work through a text they are also working through varied purposes for reading. (This means you'll need to have an ample supply of all role sheets available in the room at all times. Color coding is helpful, through unecological.) Some of our Chicago-area teachers have experimented with having kids stay with just one role throughout a book, but the results haven't been great. They report that energy drops around the middle of the book, and they feel disappointed that kids don't get a chance to internalize different roles. Some teachers even feel that having kids stick to one role postpones the time when everyone can abandon the role sheets altogether.

Discarded Roles

Many of us who have experimented with literature circles started out using one additional role, drawn directly from the literature of collaborative learning, called *process checker*. This person's role is to monitor and rate the other members of the group on the quality of their participation at each day's meeting. The teacher can collect this sheet as a way, among other things, of evaluating the kids' performance in circles on any given day. But many of us were uncomfortable with this role right from the start. In the first place, it made one group member into more of a cop than a kid; it lent a kind of authoritarian tone to the proceedings. More importantly, the process checker role was the only one that *did not help set purposes for reading.* All the other roles offer guidance for students *while* they read and make notes for an upcoming session. Process checkers don't go to work until the meeting begins. In the classroom, kids sometimes translated this role into a "day off." We noticed that kids getting the process checker sheet were less likely than others to do their reading in advance. Given all these drawbacks, plus the burst of better role ideas we were receiving from colleagues, many of the teachers around here threw the PC role out. Marline Pearson took another approach, turning the process checker role into an extra, separate sheet that *everyone* periodically fills out, as a way of reflecting back on the group's process.

Finally, we want to note that this problem applies across the curriculum, in any other application of cooperative learning in which a process checker (or similar) role pops up. Kids don't need a turncoat in their midst to ensure that they work: they need a good assortment of real roles that give them different purposes for preparing and different ways of beginning a conversation. Then—and only then—do they need official and constructive ways to self-evaluate their work.

Scheduling

Because literature circles are a way of enacting scaffolded learning—and for about a hundred other good reasons—they need to meet on a regular, frequent, predictable schedule. Ideally, *two to four hours a week* should be set aside for literature circles—including time for reading, preparing role sheets, and meeting in groups. If this sounds like a big chunk of time, remember two things:

1. You are trying to replace less effective activities with a *more effective* one. If literature circles do build kids' comprehension, thinking, and engagement with literature, you'll have no regrets about reallocating this much time.
2. You are making a *long-term investment* in a fundamental, recurrent activity.

Once kids really learn this structure, when they have fully internalized its norms and procedures, you can "save time" in a couple of ways. For one thing, if other events press in, you can "mothball" literature circles for a week or two, bringing them back later with confidence that kids can get right back in the groove. Some teachers call these two- or three-week patterns "cycles"—they'll do a cycle of lit circles, then a cycle of a curriculum unit, then lit circles again, or perhaps a cycle of writing workshop.

Another scheduling variation, which we'll discuss in a minute, is allocating class time for *group meetings only*, leaving the reading and role sheet work for homework. Indeed, for departmentalized middle and high school teachers, who must often deliver a huge mandated English curriculum in forty- or fifty-minute daily periods, such time adjustments may be necessary. However, even for high school classes, a more intensive and regular schedule is absolutely required for the initial training period. You cannot learn lit circles effectively if you do them only one day a week.

You'll enjoy the greatest certainty of success if you schedule in-class time for all the lit circle activities, at least at the start. Prematurely sending kids off to read and do their sheets as homework invites problems. You can count on a few kids coming to their group without the book or being unprepared for their role or just "spacing out" the whole thing. You are then guaranteed management problems that, though not overwhelming, decrease the energy in the room. Better to start by doing the whole cycle in class, where you can make sure everyone is ready and can provide immediate help.

To make this happen, many teachers divide the week into reading days and meeting days. Here's how Marianne Flanagan fits literature circles into her week in fifth grade:

Self-Contained Elementary Classroom

Monday	Tuesday	Wednesday	Thursday	Friday
10:15–11:00 Groups meet	10:15–11:00 Read & roles or logs	10:15–11:00 Groups meet	10:15–11:00 Read & roles or logs	10:15–11:00 Groups meet

Using this plan, kids have two sessions a week for reading and note writing and three for meeting. When Marianne wants kids to read longer chunks of books between meetings, she can schedule two or only one meeting a week, with more reading time in between.

If the kids are younger—say, *primary* level—they probably couldn't stay on just one task for the whole time, so many teachers divide each daily session into some reading time and some talking time, like this:

Monday	Tuesday	Wednesday	Thursday	Friday
10:15–10:30 Read & roles	10:15–10:30 Read & roles	10:15–10:30 Read & roles	10:15–10:30 Read & roles	10:15–10:30 Read & roles
10:30–10:45 Groups meet	10:30–10:45 Groups meet	10:30–10:45 Groups meet	10:30–10:45 Groups meet	10:30–10:45 Groups meet

When school becomes departmentalized, innovation gets tougher and time gets tighter. Sometimes it feels as though our secondary schools were designed to *prevent* coherent, ongoing, student-centered activities. Teachers are under such enormous time and curriculum "coverage" pressure that they feel guilty about spending even a few minutes of class time on something not officially mandated—or something not certain to succeed. Nevertheless, creative middle and high school teachers have solved this problem aptly, and here are a couple of the most common schedules:

Middle School with Double-Period Language Arts/Reading

	Monday	Tuesday	Wednesday	Thursday	Friday
8:15–9:00 *Period A*	English*	English	English	English	English
9:00–9:45 *Period B***	LC Groups meet	LC Read & roles	LC Groups meet	LC Read & roles	LC Groups meet

*"English" stands for the mandated curriculum, including teacher-guided lessons on required books, writing, etc.

**Once the lit circles are well established, the B Period schedule can alternate in two- or three-week *cycles* with writing workshop or other activities that require long, regular chunks of time.

High School Language Arts (Single Period)

Phase One: Training
Temporarily allocates *all* class time to literature circles for training. This means daily for two weeks, alternating between group meetings and reading sessions, the same as the middle school Period B above.

	Monday	Tuesday	Wednesday	Thursday	Friday
1:00–1:45	LC Groups meet	LC Read & roles	LC Groups meet	LC Read & roles	LC Groups meet

Phase Two: Long-Term Implementation
Now lit circles can be spun off as a once-a-week activity, with reading and role sheets done as homework.

	Monday	Tuesday	Wednesday	Thursday	Friday
8:15–9:00	English*	English	English	English	LC

*"English" stands for the rest of the mandated curriculum, including teacher-guided lessons on required books, writing, etc.

Each of these schedules assumes that the whole class works on literature circles at once, in perhaps five or six groups. Of course, it is also possible to have only *one circle meet at a time,* while other students read, write, conduct peer conferences, do some math, visit centers, or are otherwise productively engaged. However, when only one lit circle meets at a time it is usually because *the teachers are running the groups.* They cannot comfortably let all the groups meet simultaneously. Such teachers feel a need to be present in each group, to supervise, and all too often, to take over. They clearly aren't yet attuned to the dynamics—or trusting of the power—of genuine kid-led collaborative learning.

The problem here—as in many classrooms where lit circles are being tried—is confusion between time devoted to teacher-directed and student-sponsored reading. In teasing apart this puzzle, let's look back at the classroom that began this book—Karen Smith's fifth-grade room in Phoenix. After working with her emergent literature studies for a few years, Karen settled on a pattern whereby students worked in kid-run groups for three weeks per month and then joined in a group with her for one week per month, to read a book together. In this teacher-and-kid-directed literature study, Karen was a fellow reader, but she also prepared carefully and dug deep to help individual kids excavate meaning and connect with the author's craft. This meant that during this stretch of Karen's school day, kids were guided by the teacher about one-fourth of the time, while during the other three-fourths they pursued their reading as individuals in kid-run groups. Karen's is the essence of a balanced curriculum—and the process of structuring that three-fourths student-sponsored time is what this book is mainly about.

The Importance of Ending Dates

Because we value some time for sharing between groups when books are finished, and because we want groups to swap members extensively after each book, it is important to have ending dates. There's nothing complicated about this: at the start of a cycle, the kids and the teacher estimate how long it will take for everyone to finish the books, and they establish a common completion date. The length of time needed will depend heavily on the amount of in-class reading and meeting time the teacher has scheduled, of course. With intermediate through high school kids, two to three weeks seems to be a common time frame; with the younger ones and their shorter books, the cycle is often much quicker. The finishing date also provides natural pressure for groups to budget their reading assignments

liscussion schedule carefully, making sure the book is divided evenly
and will be done on time. Another handy side effect is that the faster readers
(who will generally choose longer, harder books) will be reading more pages
per day, and the slower readers (who typically pick shorter, easier books)
will be reading fewer. Still, in this kind of unobtrusive, "natural individualization," *everyone* reads and discusses a whole book each cycle.

Sharing Sessions

At the end of the cycle, each group figures out a way to share their
reading with others in the classroom. At one level, this is a way for the
readers to pull together their thinking about a book, to celebrate and culminate their reading. But this is also a vital form of "advertising" in the
classroom; these reports are one of the main ways that students hear about
books they might like to read—or avoid—when the next cycle begins. The
sharing, which often lasts for one or two days every couple of weeks, also
provides a nice change of pace, a coming together, an opportunity for
students to discuss, perform, or connect their readings.

The scope and formality of this sharing, as well as the time devoted
to it, can vary. Many teachers advise groups to finish their book a day or
two before the end of the cycle so they'll have time to plan and prepare
their product or presentation. If more days are allocated and the cycle is
stretched accordingly, then kids can create more formal, polished reports—
but they will ultimately be doing less reading. Evaluating students' sharing
presents similar choices. Depending on the teacher's judgment (or the grading policies of the school), kids can create projects as a group, prepare a
multipart product or performance in which each student is responsible for
one component, or do individual projects. Although regular book reports
are possible outcomes, they certainly violate the playful spirit of literature
circles. Among the sharing devices used by kids in our literature circle
network are:

> Posters advertising the book.
> Siskel-and-Ebert-type review "duels."
> Readers theater performances.
> Performances of a "lost scene" from the book.
> A sequel to the story.
> Read-alouds of key passages (with discussion and commentaries).

Videotaped dramatizations.

A time line of the story.

Panel debates.

Reader-on-the-street interviews (live or videotaped).

Report on the author's life.

A new ending for the book.

A new character for the book.

Collages representing different characters.

An artwork—painting, sculpture, poem, mobile, collage, diorama—interpreting the book.

An original skit based on the book.

A new cover for the book.

An advertising campaign for the book.

Diary of a character.

Diorama of a key scene.

Letter recommending the book to the acquisitions librarian.

Impersonation of a character (in costume, with props).

Interview with the author (real or fictionalized).

Interview with a character.

Letters to (or from) a character.

The story rewritten for younger kids as a picture book.

Plans for a party for all the characters in the book.

A song or a dance about the book.

News broadcast reporting events from the book.

Family tree of a key character.

Gravestone and eulogy for a character.

A puppet show about the book.

A board game based on the book.

Background/research on the setting or period.

• • • • • • • • • •

CHAPTER FIVE

Materials and Role Sheets

WHILE LITERATURE circles are a quite elegant and sophisticated classroom activity, they are not dependent on equipment. Teachers who want to get started won't require any exotic, high-tech materials. What they will need is lots of *books*—fiction and nonfiction—as well as articles, magazines, and other printed materials. Because *choice* is such a key element of literature circles, teachers must provide plenty of real reading alternatives in the classroom (or quickly available outside). And those choices need to be available in sets of four to six copies of the same text, so that groups can be formed around kids' preferences.

Sometimes, of course, the teacher will prefer literature circles where all groups read the same book, or pick from a small set of preselected choices. This may be done either for training purposes or to hook literature circles into a chunk of required curriculum. These variations are, with certain cautions, perfectly valid, and we will address each of them later. For now, however, we're going to concentrate on "basic," student-directed literature circles, mainly used in language arts classes, structured around wide, genuine student choice.

Very few teachers actually begin literature circles with a huge classroom library already in place. Traditional American schools provide teachers with quite a different assortment of reading resources: typically, book money goes for classroom sets of thick, costly textbooks and anthologies, and single copies of "real" literature are then ordered for the library. So the first challenge for would-be literature circlers is to get a few sets of attractive titles into the classroom, so kids will have something to pick from. Still, you don't need a five-thousand-volume classroom library to *begin* using literature circles. Though it obviously limits kids' choices in an absolute sense, most teachers actually start with four to six copies of a handful of titles—perhaps only enough to total the number of kids in class. What this essentially says to the kids is: "You gotta pick *one* of these six books to read. But isn't that better than getting only one choice?"

Most teachers should be able to assemble this kind of rudimentary library, at least temporarily, through several sources. First, they can work with their *school or public librarian,* checking out multiple copies of promising titles. They can also borrow sets of books from *other teachers* or from the school *bookroom,* where leftover/unused copies of novels often accumulate. Enterprising teachers can also look outside the building for sets of books. Marianne Flanagan, whom we met earlier, wrote and won a $300 *grant* during her first year of literature circles, which brought more than twenty-five sets into her room in one purchase. Some progressive school districts are beginning to spend their *book budgets* in new ways. In Orland Park, Illinois, with the active support of the superintendent and curriculum director, the district stopped purchasing most of the workbooks, black-line masters, activity kits, and other assorted "consumables" that accompany the adopted basal series—and then shifted the leftover money to classroom libraries selected by teachers. Indeed, committed teachers need not wait for their own districts to follow suit—they should officially request new budget allocations, sending memos and proposals through the appropriate channels, so that kids get the books they really need.

Until book-buying priorities shift in American schools, however, it is likely that most lit circle teachers will continue to be part-time scavengers, prowling garage sales (where ten cents a copy is not an uncommon price), saving up book-club points, soliciting donations from the PTA/PTO, running bake-a-book sales, and otherwise building their collections. As a classroom library grows, however, it starts exerting a magical magnetic power on other books in the area. Books just seem to flow to the classroom. As other people—parents, friends, community members, ex-students—become aware that a beloved teacher is collecting books, donations happen. It turns out, quite happily, that the world is full of books that need a new home and new readers.

Special sources of books for elementary teachers are the children's book clubs—Tab, Trumpet, Scholastic, and others—which sell their wares through monthly newsletters distributed to school kids. Teachers' payoff for abetting this crafty capitalist caper is "points," credits that can be spent for free books for the classroom. And since the prices charged by most clubs are very, very low, teachers can get lots of books for a few points. Copies of out-of-copyright classics (*Huckleberry Finn, War of the Worlds,* etc.) often go for as little as $1.50. While these flimsy paperback editions are only good for perhaps a half-dozen readings, they're still a cheap way to build a library fast. Shrewd teachers heartily support the children's book clubs: they encourage their kids' parents to buy plenty of books when each order form comes out—or even to buy a book or two for the whole class, not just their own child.

Levels

As teachers select sets of books for a classroom library, they consider not just the interests but the *reading levels* of their students. After all, one of the wonderful built-in features of literature circles is that they can provide natural individualization in the classroom. When a kid selects a book, she is putting herself into a temporary, appropriately leveled reading group. Of course, all this book choosing works best when kids have plenty of chances to peruse a book before they commit to it: having books on display for flip-throughs, hearing the teacher give a brief "book chat," or reading the posters or book reviews prepared by circles who've previously read the book.

Given a good assortment of subjects, authors, and difficulty levels, kids will usually group themselves wisely: in general, they'll pick books they can read comfortably and want to read. But sometimes, if the subject matter—or the other kids in the group—are really appealing, students may pick a title that's tougher than their usual comfort level. At other times, kids may also pick down, enjoying a really easy book on a topic of special interest. Literature circles automatically mix kids up in constantly shifting groupings, so that everyone gets to know and work with everyone, without the usual rigid classifications of high, low, or middle. The structure invites safe, comfortable experimenting and risk taking among developing readers.

Clipboards

When it's 9:30 in Sandy King's third-grade class, that means it's "lit circle time." Without a cue from Sandy, all the children start pulling their novels and *clipboards* out of their desks. Grinning and looking quite official, these twenty-six eight-year-olds march off to their current groups, happily toting the tools of their new trade.

One of the simplest ways of concretizing some key norms of literature circles is to issue students a clipboard, which they bring to each circle meeting with their role sheet for the day attached. This means that kids go off to their group with two things—the book they're reading and their prepared ideas for the discussion, ready to go. The clipboard also has some nice symbolic properties—it implies an organized, businesslike approach that the younger ones especially seem to enjoy. On a more practical note, having a clipboard makes it possible to jot notes no matter where you're sitting—in a circle of chairs, on the reading rug, on the hallway floor. Because literature circles are a fairly noisy activity and groups need to get some separation from each other, it becomes operationally quite helpful if, wherever groups form, kids are able to write. Clipboards solve that problem.

Post-it Notes and Bookmarks

Eric Paulsen, who teaches fourth grade in Highland Park, Illinois, got excited about literature circles the first time he heard about them, so he printed up some role sheets and plunged in. While his kids liked the activity immediately, they experienced some problems. These nine-year-olds were having a hard time relocating important items they had found during their reading, things they had planned to share with their groups. The vocabulary enrichers couldn't quickly find their chosen words, the literary luminaries would lose track of their favorite read-alouds, and so forth. While the preprinted role sheets (like those later in this chapter) did include blanks that reminded kids to record the location of chosen items, filling in these blanks became a tangle and a bore.

Wanting a simpler and more concrete solution, Eric thought of Post-it notes. Giving kids a supply of the smallest (one-inch-square) variety, he asked them to flag the items, placing the note so it "underlined" the item they wanted to mark and leaving an edge sticking out of the book as an easy marker. He also reminded kids that they could write on the sticky note—either an arrow pointing directly at a given word or phrase in the text, or a few words to remind themselves what they wanted to say to their group. Now, Eric says, his kids' discussions run much more smoothly— fewer of those awkward, energy-sapping moments when group members paw through their books trying to find lost ideas.

As veteran primary teachers Ann Paziotopoulos and Marianne Kroll know very well, younger kids need special help in remembering the parts of a book that they want to share with friends later. Their invention is to supply kids with *bookmarks*—either blank ones, which basically work like Post-its, or premade sets, labeled and illustrated with topics kids are likely to want to mark and share. For example, Ann and Marianne have a set of bookmarks for mysteries that includes Clue, Crime, Detective, Criminal, Victim, and Setting. Kids in their classes can simply use the appropriate bookmark to mark a section of the book—or they can use blanks and make their own.

Role Logs and Hats

At Shabonee School in Northbrook, Judith Epcke devised a neat adaptation that saved copying all those role sheets *and* paved the way for individual reading response logs. First Judy took her class through a couple of cycles of literature circles using regular role sheets. Then, once the kids had internalized the job of each role, she gave out a *spiral notebook* for each role in each group. Now when kids jot their notes for the next LC meeting, they write in the official spiral for their assigned role. Later, they come to the group and talk from their notes. After the discussion, the kids swap spirals and take home the one for their next role, and so on. One neat outcome of this procedure is that all previous connectors' or discussion directors' comments are collected in one volume. This makes it very simple for the teacher to review the work of a group by reading and correlating the entries in four or five notebooks.

One idea we've used mostly for fun in teacher-training sessions is a set of multicolored baseball *hats*, each one with a lit circle role jauntily embroidered on it. Somehow, it's terrific to look across the group and see one of your partners wearing an electric-green "Discussion Director" or neon-pink "Illustrator" hat. And the hats serve as a visual reminder of what role each person is supposed to take. (Of course, you could accomplish the same thing with a one-cent nametag, but this is much more special.) We haven't heard of any classroom teachers who've bought a class set of this particular audiovisual aid—at $12 to $15 a hat, you can buy a lot of books for the same money. But if you've got deep pockets or a grant, you can order these custom-lettered hats from all sorts of mail order catalogs and some sporting good stores. We've even seen a booth at a local fair where a guy with a huge embroidering machine makes them for you on the spot.

Reading Response Logs

The role sheets described in this chapter are transitional, temporary devices: the goal of role sheets is to make role sheets obsolete. We use them to help students internalize and practice taking multiple cognitive perspectives on texts. In many classrooms, the role sheets are abandoned as soon as groups are capable of lively, text-centered, multifaceted discussions. Then the teacher invites kids to record their responses and discussion ideas, during or after reading, in open-ended personal literature response logs. This fully opens up the possibility that kids will bring not just one kind of response but several—perhaps a drawing, a couple of questions, and a connection or two.

When are kids ready to drop the roles and move to response logs? It usually requires using the roles for a while, getting in the habit of adopting a half-dozen different angles on reading, amassing a repertoire of group discussion roles, and practicing within a safe structure until less guidance is needed. Once kids have had plenty of successful group meetings, the structured roles are probably unnecessary, and wise teachers will phase them out quickly. After all, the goal of literature circles is to have natural and sophisticated discussions of literature—once that is happening, who needs handouts?

Role Sheets

Other than the books themselves, the most important equipment for literature circles are the *role sheets,* which give a different thinking task to each group member. On the pages that follow are some of the roles that teachers in our network have used successfully. All of these role sheets are designed to enact the key principles of collaborative learning and to initiate a genuine, kid-led, self-sustaining discussion. (For ideas on *group size, selecting roles, scheduling, and managing groups,* see Chapters 3 and 4. Some of the more common problems teachers have encountered and solved are discussed in Chapter 10.)

Sample Role Sheets

The four sets of role sheets presented here have been developed and used by some of the contributing teachers you've met in this book.

However, we think of these as "generic" sets, and almost everyone who does literature circles has a personalized version.

Set A — Eight all-purpose, basic roles for fiction
Set B — Five basic roles for nonfiction (these may be supplemented with Roles 5, 7, and 8 from Set A)
Set C — Five roles for primary students
Set D — Eight Spanish role sheets for primary/intermediate students, prepared by Bonnie Barelli of Tioga Elementary School
Set E — Two special roles for jigsawing and for heterogeneous groups

While readers of this book are entirely welcome to copy these role sheets for classroom use, teachers may find it even more helpful to design their own job sheets, with help from their students.

Name _____

Group _____

Book _____

Assignment p _____–p _____

Discussion Director: Your job is to develop a list of questions that your group might want to discuss about this part of the book. Don't worry about the small details: your task is to help people talk over the big ideas in the reading and share their reactions. Usually the best discussion questions come from your own thoughts, feelings, and concerns as you read, which you can list below, during or after your reading. Or you may use some of the general questions below to develop topics for your group.

Possible discussion questions or topics for today:

1. _____

2. _____

3. _____

4. _____

5. _____

Sample questions:

What was going through your mind while you read this?

How did you feel while reading this part of the book?

What was discussed in this section of the book?

Can someone summarize briefly?

Did today's reading remind you of any real-life experiences?

What questions did you have when you finished this section?

Did anything in this section of the book surprise you?

What are the one or two most important ideas?

Predict some things you think will be talked about next.

Topic to be carried over to tomorrow _____

Assignment for tomorrow p _____–p _____

From *Literature Circles: Voice and choice in the student-centered classroom* by Harvey Daniels. Stenhouse Publishers, York, ME.

Name _____

Group _____

Book _____

Assignment p _____–p _____

Literary Luminary: Your job is to locate a few special sections of the text that your group would like to hear read aloud. The idea is to help people remember some interesting, powerful, funny, puzzling, or important sections of the text. You decide which passages or paragraphs are worth hearing, and then jot plans for how they should be shared. You can read passages aloud yourself, ask someone else to read them, or have people read them silently and then discuss.

Location	Reason for Picking	Plan for Reading
1. Page _____	_____	_____
Paragraph _____	_____	_____
2. Page _____	_____	_____
Paragraph _____	_____	_____
3. Page _____	_____	_____
Paragraph _____	_____	_____
4. Page _____	_____	_____
Paragraph _____	_____	_____

Possible reasons for picking a passage to be shared:

Important   Informative
Surprising   Controversial
Funny   Well written
Confusing   Thought-provoking

Other:

_____

_____

Topic to be carried over to tomorrow _____

Assignment for tomorrow p _____–p _____

Name _____

Group _____

Book _____

Assignment p _____–p _____

Illustrator: Your job is to draw some kind of picture related to the reading. It can be a sketch, cartoon, diagram, flow chart, or stick-figure scene. You can draw a picture of something that's discussed specifically in your book, or something that the reading reminded you of, or a picture that conveys any idea or feeling you got from the reading. Any kind of drawing or graphic is okay—you can even label things with words if that helps. **Make your drawing on the other side of this sheet or on a separate sheet.**

Presentation plan: When the Discussion Director invites your participation, you may show your picture without comment to the others in the group. One at a time, they get to speculate what your picture means, to connect the drawing to their own ideas about the reading. After everyone has had a say, you get the last word: tell them what your picture means, where it came from, or what it represents to you.

Topic to be carried over to tomorrow _____

Assignment for tomorrow p _____–p _____

From *Literature Circles: Voice and choice in the student-centered classroom* by Harvey Daniels. Stenhouse Publishers, York, ME.

Name _____

Group _____

Book _____

Assignment p _____–p _____

Connector: Your job is to find connections between the book your group is reading and the world outside. This means connecting the reading to your own life, to happenings at school or in the community, to similar events at other times and places, to other people or problems that you are reminded of. You might also see connections between this book and other writings on the same topic, or by the same author. There are no right answers here—whatever the reading connects **you** with is worth sharing!

Some connections I found between this reading and other people, places, events, authors . . .

1. _____

_____

2. _____

_____

3. _____

_____

4. _____

_____

5. _____

_____

Topic to be carried over to tomorrow _____

Assignment for tomorrow p _____–p _____

From *Literature Circles: Voice and choice in the student-centered classroom* by Harvey Daniels. Stenhouse Publishers, York, ME.

Name _____

Group _____

Book _____

Assignment p _____–p _____

Summarizer: Your job is to prepare a brief summary of today's reading. The other members of your group will be counting on you to give a quick (one- or two-minute) statement that conveys the gist, the key points, the main highlights, the **essence** of today's reading assignment. If there are several main ideas or events to remember, you can use the numbered slots below.

Summary:

_____

_____

_____

_____

Key points:

1. _____

2. _____

3. _____

4. _____

5. _____

Topic to be carried over to tomorrow _____

Assignment for tomorrow p _____–p _____

From *Literature Circles: Voice and choice in the student-centered classroom* by Harvey Daniels. Stenhouse Publishers, York, ME.

VOCABULARY ENRICHER

Name _____

Group _____

Book _____

Assignment p _____–p _____

Vocabulary Enricher: Your job is to be on the lookout for a few especially important **words** in today's reading. If you find words that are puzzling or unfamiliar, mark them while you are reading, and then later jot down their definition, either from a dictionary or some other source. You may also run across familiar words that stand out somehow in the reading—words that are repeated a lot, used in an unusual way, or key to the meaning of the text. Mark these special words too, and be ready to point them out to the group. When your circle meets, help members find and discuss these words.

Page No. & Paragraph	Word	Definition	Plan
_____	_____	_____	_____
_____	_____	_____	_____
_____	_____	_____	_____
_____	_____	_____	_____
_____	_____	_____	_____

Topic to be carried over to tomorrow _____

Assignment for tomorrow p _____–p _____

From *Literature Circles: Voice and choice in the student-centered classroom* by Harvey Daniels. Stenhouse Publishers, York, ME.

Name _____

Group _____

Book _____

Assignment p _____–p _____

Travel Tracer: When you are reading a book where characters move around a lot and the scene changes frequently, it is important for everyone in your group to know **where** things are happening and how the setting may have changed. So that's your job: to track carefully where the action takes place during today's reading. Describe each setting in detail, either in words or with an action map or diagram you can show to your group. Be sure to give the page locations where the scene is described.

Describe or sketch the setting (you may also use the back of this sheet or another sheet):

Where today's action **begins:**   Page where it is described _____

_____

_____

Where **key events** happen today: Page where it is described _____

_____

_____

Where today's events **end:**   Page where it is described _____

_____

_____

Topic to be carried over to tomorrow _____

Assignment for tomorrow p _____–p _____

INVESTIGATOR

Name _____

Group _____

Book _____

Assignment p _____–p _____

Investigator: Your job is to dig up some background information on any topic related to your book. This might include:

The geography, weather, culture, or history of the book's setting.
Information about the author, her/his life, and other works.
Information about the time period portrayed in the book.
Pictures, objects, or materials that illustrate elements of the book.
The history and derivation of words or names used in the book.
Music that reflects the book or the time.

This is **not** a formal research report. The idea is to find one bit of information or material that helps your group understand the book better. Investigate something that really interests you—something that struck you as puzzling or curious while you were reading.

Ways of gathering information:

The introduction, preface, or "about the author" section of the book.
Library books and magazines.
On-line computer search or encyclopedia.
Interviews with people who know the topic.
Other novels, nonfiction, or textbooks you've read.

Topic to be carried over to tomorrow _____

Assignment for tomorrow p _____–p _____

From *Literature Circles: Voice and choice in the student-centered classroom* by Harvey Daniels. Stenhouse Publishers, York, ME.

Name _____

Group _____

Book _____

Assignment p _____–p _____

Discussion Director: Your job is to develop a list of questions that your group might want to discuss about today's reading. Don't worry about the small details: your task is to help people talk over the big ideas in the reading and share reactions. Usually the best discussion questions come from your own thoughts, feelings, and concerns as you read, which you can list below, during or after your reading. Or you may use some of the general questions below to develop topics for your group.

Possible discussion questions or topics for today:

1. _____

2. _____

3. _____

4. _____

5. _____

Sample questions:

What was going through your mind while you read this?
How did you feel?
What were you reminded of?
What was discussed here? Can someone summarize briefly?
What questions did you have when you finished this selection?
Did anything surprise you?
What are the one or two most important ideas?
Predict some things you think will be talked about next.

Topic to be carried over to tomorrow _____

Assignment for tomorrow p _____–p _____

PASSAGE MASTER (NONFICTION)

Name _____

Group _____

Book _____

Assignment p _____–p _____

Passage Master: Your job is to locate a few special sections of the reading that the group should look back on. The idea is to help people notice the most interesting, funny, puzzling, or important sections of the text. You decide which passages or paragraphs are worth reviewing and then jot plans for how they should be shared with the group. You can read passages aloud yourself, ask someone else to read them, or have people read them silently and then discuss.

Location	Reason for Picking	Plan for Reading
1. Page ____	_____	_____
Paragraph ____	_____	_____
2. Page ____	_____	_____
Paragraph ____	_____	_____
3. Page ____	_____	_____
Paragraph ____	_____	_____
4. Page ____	_____	_____
Paragraph ____	_____	_____

Possible reasons for picking a passage to be shared:

Important   Informative
Surprising   Controversial
Funny   Well written
Confusing   Thought-provoking

Other:

_____

_____

Topic to be carried over to tomorrow _____

Assignment for tomorrow p _____–p _____

From *Literature Circles: Voice and choice in the student-centered classroom* by Harvey Daniels. Stenhouse Publishers, York, ME.

Name _____

Group _____

Book _____

Assignment p _____–p _____

Vocabulary Enricher: Your job is to be on the lookout for a few especially important words—new, interesting, strange, important, puzzling, or unfamiliar words—words that members of the group need to notice and understand. Mark some of these key words while you are reading, and then later jot down their definition, either from the text or from a dictionary or other source. In the group, help members find and discuss these words.

Page No. & Paragraph	Word	Definition	Plan
_____	_____	_____	_____
_____	_____	_____	_____
_____	_____	_____	_____
_____	_____	_____	_____
_____	_____	_____	_____
_____	_____	_____	_____

Topic to be carried over to tomorrow _____

Assignment for tomorrow p _____–p _____

From *Literature Circles: Voice and choice in the student-centered classroom* by Harvey Daniels. Stenhouse Publishers, York, ME.

Name _____

Group _____

Book _____

Assignment p _____–p _____

Illustrator: Your job is to draw some kind of picture related to the reading. It can be a sketch, cartoon, diagram, flow chart, or stick-figure scene. You can draw a picture of something that's discussed specifically in the text, or something that the reading reminded you of, or a picture that conveys any idea or feeling you got from the reading. Any sort of drawing or graphic representation is okay—you can even label things with words if that helps. **Make your drawing on the other side of this sheet or on a separate sheet.**

Presentation plan: When the Discussion Director invites your participation, you may show your picture without comment to the others in the group. One at a time, they get to speculate what your picture means, to connect the drawing to their own ideas about the reading and the subject at hand. After everyone has had a say, you get the last word: you get to tell them what your picture means, where it came from, or what it represents to you.

Topic to be carried over to tomorrow _____

Assignment for tomorrow p _____–p _____

From *Literature Circles: Voice and choice in the student-centered classroom* by Harvey Daniels. Stenhouse Publishers, York, ME.

Name _____

Group _____

Book _____

Assignment p _____–p _____

Connector: Your job is to find connections between the material your group is reading and the world outside. This means connecting the reading to your own life, to happenings at school or in the community, to similar events at other times and places, to other people or problems that you are reminded of. You might also see connections between this material and other writings on the same topic, or by the same author. There are no right answers here—whatever the reading connects **you** with is worth sharing!

Some connections I found between this reading and other people, places, events, authors . . .

1. _____

_____

2. _____

_____

3. _____

_____

4. _____

_____

5. _____

_____

Topic to be carried over to tomorrow _____

Assignment for tomorrow p _____–p _____

From *Literature Circles: Voice and choice in the student-centered classroom* by Harvey Daniels. Stenhouse Publishers, York, ME.

DISCUSSION DIRECTOR

Name _____

Group _____

Book _____

Assignment p _____–p _____

You are the **Discussion Director.** Your job is to write down some good questions that you think your group would want to talk about.

1. _____

_____

_____

2. _____

_____

_____

3. Why . . .

4. How . . .

5. If . . .

From *Literature Circles: Voice and choice in the student-centered classroom* by Harvey Daniels. Stenhouse Publishers, York, ME.

Name _____

Group _____

Book _____

Assignment p _____–p _____

You are the **Passage Picker.** Your job is to pick parts of the story that you want to read aloud to your group. These can be:

—a good part   —an interesting part
—a funny part   —some good writing
—a scary part   —a good description

Be sure to mark the parts you want to share with a Post-it note or bookmark. Or you can write on this sheet the parts you want to share.

Parts to read out loud:

Page	Paragraph	Why I liked it
____	_____	_____
____	_____	_____
____	_____	_____
____	_____	_____
____	_____	_____

From *Literature Circles: Voice and choice in the student-centered classroom* by Harvey Daniels. Stenhouse Publishers, York, ME.

Name _____

Group _____

Book _____

Assignment p _____–p _____

You are the **Artful Artist.** Your job is to draw anything about the story that you liked:

—a character
—the setting
—a problem
—an exciting part
—a surprise
—a prediction of what will happen next
—anything else

Draw on the back of this page or on a bigger piece of paper if you need it. Do any kind of drawing or picture you like.

When your group meets, don't tell what your drawing is. Let them guess and talk about it first. Then you can tell about it.

From *Literature Circles: Voice and choice in the student-centered classroom* by Harvey Daniels. Stenhouse Publishers, York, ME.

Name _____

Group _____

Book _____

Assignment p _____–p _____

You are the **Word Finder.** Your job is to look for special words in the story. Words that are:

—new   —interesting
—different   —important
—strange   —hard
—funny

When you find a word that you want to talk about, mark it with a Post-it note or write it down here.

Word	Page	Why I picked it
_____	____	_____
		_____
_____	____	_____
		_____
		_____
_____	____	_____
		_____
_____	____	_____
		_____
_____	____	_____
		_____

When your group meets, help your friends talk about the words you have chosen. Things you can discuss:

How does this word fit in the story?
Does anyone know what this word means?
Shall we look it up in the dictionary?
What does this word make you feel like?
Can you draw the word?

From *Literature Circles: Voice and choice in the student-centered classroom* by Harvey Daniels. Stenhouse Publishers, York, ME.

Name _____

Group _____

Book _____

Assignment p _____ –p _____

You are the **Connector.** Your job is to find connections between the book and the world outside. This means connecting the reading to:

—your own life
—happenings at school or in the neighborhood
—similar events at other times and places
—other people or problems
—other books or stories
—other writings on the same topics
—other writings by the same author

Some things today's reading reminded me of were . . .

From *Literature Circles: Voice and choice in the student-centered classroom* by Harvey Daniels. Stenhouse Publishers, York, ME.

Nombre _____

Grupo _____

Título _____

He leído de la página _____ **a la página** _____

Ud. es el director/directora de la charla. Su trabajo es formular buenas preguntas para poder hablar en su grupo. (Use el cubo de las preguntas para ayudarle.)

Preguntas para hoy:

1. _____

_____

2. _____

_____

3. _____

_____

4. _____

_____

5. _____

_____

Nombre _____

Grupo _____

Título _____

He leído de la página _____ **a la página** _____

Ud. es el artista talentoso. Dibuje una parte del cuento que le haya gustado mucho.

Personajes:

_____

_____

_____

Lugar (donde ocurre el cuento):

_____

_____

_____

Problema:

_____

_____

_____

Solución:

_____

_____

_____

Parte favorita:

_____

_____

_____

No hable de su dibujo hasta que el resto del grupo esté preparado para compartir. Los otros compañeros tienen que tratar de adivinar lo que dibujó.

From *Literature Circles: Voice and choice in the student-centered classroom* by Harvey Daniels. Stenhouse Publishers, York, ME.

Nombre _____

Grupo _____

Título _____

He leído de la página _____ **a la página** _____

Su trabajo es encontrar los enlaces entre el libro que está leyendo y todo lo que está a su alrededor. Este libro me hace pensar sobre . . .

. . . un libro que he leído antes

. . . un lugar que he visto antes

. . . algo que me pasó a mí, a mi familia, a mis amigos

. . . personajes de otros libros

. . . películas que he visto

. . . cosas que pasaron en la escuela, en casa o en el vecindario

From *Literature Circles: Voice and choice in the student-centered classroom* by Harvey Daniels. Stenhouse Publishers, York, ME.

Nombre _____

Grupo _____

Título _____

He leído de la página _____ **a la página** _____

Ud. tiene que conocer y entender a los personajes del libro. Describa las personalidades—como se comportan. Describa como se sienten. ¿Qué están pensando?

¿Son los personajes como Ud., como alguien de su familia, o como personas que Ud. conoce?

Yo pienso:

_____

_____

El personaje principal (¿Quién es el personaje más importante del cuento?):

_____

_____

Haga un dibujo del personaje:

_____

_____

Otro personaje que le gustó:

_____

_____

Haga un dibujo de este personaje:

_____

_____

From *Literature Circles: Voice and choice in the student-centered classroom* by Harvey Daniels. Stenhouse Publishers, York, ME.

Nombre _____

Grupo _____

Título _____

He leído de la página _____ **a la página** _____

Ud. es el sabelotodo de las palabras. Busque diferentes partes del cuento que quiere leer en voz alta a su grupo. Busque alguna parte que . . .

. . . le haga reír

. . . le haga sentir triste

. . . relate una conversación interesante entre los personajes

. . . use descripciones vívidas

. . . le haga pensar en otras ideas, libros o cosas que le pasaron

. . . le cause curiosidad o que le haga maravillarse

From *Literature Circles: Voice and choice in the student-centered classroom* by Harvey Daniels. Stenhouse Publishers, York, ME.

Nombre _____

Grupo _____

Título _____

He leído de la página _____ **a la página** _____

Cuando se lee un libro, los personajes se cambian mucho de lugar y el ambiente cambia frecuentemente. Es importante que su grupo sepa dónde suceden las cosas y cómo cambia el ambiente. Éste es su trabajo: trazar donde pasa la acción de la lectura de hoy. Describa cada lugar en detalle con palabras o en forma de un mapa para enseñárselo a su grupo. Indique las páginas donde se describe el lugar.

Describa o dibuje el lugar donde ocurre la acción:

1. Donde empieza la acción: La página

_____   _____

_____   _____

2. Donde pasó algo importante hoy: La página

_____   _____

_____   _____

3. Donde terminó la acción de hoy: La página

_____   _____

_____   _____

From *Literature Circles: Voice and choice in the student-centered classroom* by Harvey Daniels. Stenhouse Publishers, York, ME.

Nombre _____

Grupo _____

Título _____

He leído de la página _____ **a la página** _____

Su trabajo es buscar información sobre cualquier tema que tenga algo que ver con el libro. Esto puede ser:

La geografía, el clima, la cultura, la historia del lugar donde ocurrió el cuento.
Información sobre el autor/autora, su vida y otros libros que escribió.
Información sobre el período que está representado en el cuento.

Lo importante de esta investigación es buscar información o materiales que ayuden a su grupo a comprender mejor el libro. Investigue algo muy interesante (algo que le parece curioso o interesante mientras lo esté leyendo).

Maneras para investigar:

Lea la introducción, cualquier información sobre el autor.
Lea otros libros de la biblioteca o revistas.
Haga investigaciones en las computadoras o en la enciclopedia.
Entreviste a personas que sepan sobre el tema.
Consulte otros libros de ficción, libros de información u otros libros de texto.

From *Literature Circles: Voice and choice in the student-centered classroom* by Harvey Daniels. Stenhouse Publishers, York, ME.

Nombre _____

Grupo _____

Título _____

He leído de la página _____ a la página _____

Experto: Su tarea es localizar unas cuantas secciones especiales del texto que a su grupo les gustaría escuchar. El propósito es ayudarles a recordar algunas secciones interesantes, profundas, divertidas, confusas, o importantes. Ud. decide cuales pasajes o párrafos del texto valen la pena de ser escuchados y luego escribe sus planes de como cree que tales deberían ser compartidos. Ud. podría ser la persona que lee los pasajes en voz alta; otra persona podría leerlos o miembros de su grupo podrían leer en silencio y luego hablar sobr la lectura.

Localización	Razón por la cual fue escogido	Plan de Lectura
1. Página _____	_____	_____
Párrafo _____	_____	_____
2. Página _____	_____	_____
Párrafo _____	_____	_____
3. Página _____	_____	_____
Párrafo _____	_____	_____
4. Página _____	_____	_____
Párrafo _____	_____	_____

Posibles razones por las cuales un pasaje ha sido escogido para ser compartido:

Importante	Informativo
Sorprendente	Polémico
Divertido	Bien escrito
Confuso	Provoca discusión

Otras:

_____

_____

From *Literature Circles: Voice and choice in the student-centered classroom* by Harvey Daniels. Stenhouse Publishers, York, ME.

Name _____

Group _____

Book _____

Assignment p _____–p _____

While you are reading or after you have finished reading, please prepare for the group meeting by doing the following:

Discussion questions: Jot down a few questions or topics that you would like to discuss with your group. These should come directly from **your own reaction** to the reading—what did you feel, think, notice, wonder, or want to talk about while reading?

1. _____

2. _____

3. _____

4. _____

Passages: Mark some lines or sections in the text that caught your attention—sections that somehow "jumped out" at you as you read. These might be passages that seem especially important, puzzling, beautiful, strange, well written, controversial, or striking in some other way. Be ready to read these aloud to the group, or to ask someone else to read them.

Words: Mark a few important words for your group to discuss. These might be words that are unfamiliar, new, or strange—or words that are especially central to the meaning of your text.

Illustration: On the back of this sheet, quickly sketch a picture related to your reading. This can be a drawing, cartoon, diagram, flow chart—whatever. You can draw a picture of something that's specifically talked about in the text or something from your own experience or feelings, something the reading made you think about. Be ready to show your picture to your group and talk about it.

From *Literature Circles: Voice and choice in the student-centered classroom* by Harvey Daniels. Stenhouse Publishers, York, ME.

Name _____

Group _____

Book _____

Assignment p _____–p _____

Everyone in your group is reading something different, but related. In order to have a good discussion, everyone will need to both share and connect. To prepare for your group meeting, please respond to the following four tasks, either while you read or after you have read.

Summary and reactions: Jot down a brief summary of your reading.

Author: _____

Title: _____

The main idea:_____

_____

One highlight or interesting idea you noticed:_____

_____

Your personal reaction and evaluation:_____

_____

Passages: Mark some lines or sections of the text that you could read aloud to help other group members understand your article/book.

Illustration: On the back of this sheet, quickly sketch a picture related to your reading. This can be a drawing, cartoon, diagram, flow chart—whatever. You can draw a picture of something that's specifically talked about in the text or something from your own experience or feelings, something the text made you think about. Be ready to show your picture to your group and talk about it.

Sharing plan: When the group meets, the discussion will have two stages. First, everyone will take turns identifying his or her reading by author and title and giving a quick summary and reaction. Then, everyone will join in general conversation, sharing and comparing whatever seems valuable about the readings. You can contribute your passages, illustrations, or other notes wherever they fit.

From *Literature Circles: Voice and choice in the student-centered classroom* by Harvey Daniels. Stenhouse Publishers, York, ME.

CHAPTER SIX

• • • • • • • • •

Teachers' Applications: Primary and Intermediate Grades

I have never seen a model for discussion that was so intuitive to kids, and so well liked. Most important, kids learn to trust themselves and respect each other as discussers and analysts. They bring up what is important to them, and in doing so seem to connect more deeply with the reading.

—Sharon Weiner, Baker Demonstration School

IN THIS CHAPTER and the next, fifteen classroom teachers tell how they have adopted and adapted literature circles for their students. These innovators come from a wide range of city and suburban schools, and work at grade levels from kindergarten through college. Every teacher in our network has had to refine, replan, and rearrange the student discussion groups many times—and some have had to compromise under the pressure of curriculum mandates and standardized testing. None of our models are "pure," and none of us have perfected their use. In fact, many of the accounts just ahead focus on those imperfect early days when literature circles were just getting started. But all of these different models do have a few things in common: they give kids more time to read, more choice in what they read, more opportunities to pose and pursue their own questions, more responsibility in making meaning for themselves, and more freedom to conduct their own inquiry.

A Note on Primary Literature Circles

Yes, you *can* do literature circles with primary children. The basic structure works just fine for younger kids, with a few key adaptations. As we adjust, though, we want to carefully preserve most of the defining features of true literature circles:

1. Students *choose* their own reading materials.
2. *Small temporary groups* are formed, based on book choice.
3. Different groups read *different books.*
4. Groups meet on a *regular, predictable schedule* to discuss their reading.
5. Kids use written or drawn *notes* to guide both their reading and discussion.
6. Discussion *topics come from the students.*
7. Group meetings aim to be *open, natural conversations about books,* so personal connections, digressions, and open-ended questions are welcome.
8. In newly forming groups, students play a rotating assortment of task *roles.*
9. The teacher serves as a *facilitator,* not a group member or instructor.
10. Evaluation is by *teacher observation and student self-evaluation.*
11. A spirit of *playfulness and fun* pervades the room.
12. When books are finished, *readers share with their classmates,* and then *new groups form* around new reading choices.

At Jenner School, in the heart of Chicago's Cabrini-Green housing project, Angie Bynam's thiry-two second graders meet in literature circles routinely. Angie has a large selection of picture books in multiple-copy sets that she received through a grant from the *Chicago Tribune,* and this tempting assortment of titles is displayed in face-up stacks on a large table at the back of the classroom. When it is lit circle time, Angie's kids browse through this horizontal library, gradually picking themselves into groups of four or five. This process takes a good ten minutes of searching, talking, and negotiating, and often results in kids rereading old favorites as well as venturing into new ones. As each group assembles and picks up its books, they check in at Angie's desk, where she gives out an assortment of different role sheets to members of the group.

Next, the kids push together a set of desks and take turns reading the book aloud to each other. Often, each child simply reads two facing pages, and the reader changes with each turn of a page. When the story has been read and any initial comments shared, everyone takes a few minutes to silently make notes on the role sheets that sit in front of them. After a while, the discussion director invites everyone into a conversation, and individual kids pitch in ideas about the book. As with any other well-organized literature circle, the discussion is natural, spontaneous, and wide-ranging. Sometimes the kids draw directly from their written notes and sometimes they simply talk about their personal responses to the story or the comments of other circle members. The whole process, from book selection through reading aloud, note writing, and discussion, involves about forty-five minutes of highly student-directed activity, activity few adults realize that kids at this age—or kids at this particular school—are capable of.

Like Angie Bynam, primary teachers often make adjustments in the basic literature circles model to make sure that it works with their younger students. Below are some of the variations that thoughtful primary teachers rely on:

• The *books are appropriate for emergent readers*—which means picture books, wordless books, big books, kid-made books. Like all other primary-grade reading activities, literature circles require lots of books, because the little ones burn through books fast!

• To make sure that everyone understands the story, the *books are often read aloud* to the children, either by the teacher, by other kids, by upper-grade children, by parents at home, or through tape recordings in the listening center. Obviously, the teacher needs to do some careful orchestrating to make sure everyone in a circle is ready to meet—but not let responses go "stale" while kids are waiting for a meeting.

• The *children typically read the whole book* before coming to a group discussion, rather than reading sections of the text and having several meetings, like the older kids reading chapter books. This is mainly because of the nature of the books, which are designed to be one-sitting reads.

• During or after reading, kids record their *responses in drawing or writing at their own level.* They need not fill out the differentiated role sheets used by older kids, and *all kids may use the same response format.* For the youngest kids this often means a primary version of the illustrator role: they draw a picture of "something they thought of" during the reading, and bring this drawing with them to the group as one cue for sharing. Or they may dictate their response to the teacher, aide, parent helper, or another child. For older primary children, a *reading log,* perhaps mixing writing and drawing, can be used to record impressions and ideas for sharing.

   • Even if they have drawn a picture or jotted in a log, young children often need *extra help remembering what they want to share* in the literature circle. So some teachers provide large Post-it notes for kids to mark their favorite parts of a book, encouraging them to put some words or pictures on the note to represent the response they wanted to share. Marianne Kroll and Ann Paziotopoulos provide children with sets of illustrated *bookmarks* keyed to the kind of books they are reading (the fairy tale set includes Beginning, King, Queen, Good/Evil, Ending, Magic, and Message). Kids are invited to pick just one of these bookmarks to mark a special spot in the story that they want to discuss in their group. Ann and Marianne also offer children blank bookmarks so they can illustrate their own reasons for selecting a passage to share. Putting this all together: if after reading a book, kids do some drawing or writing *and* mark some favorite spots in the text, they should be well prepared to join in a group discussion.

   • Though it is not necessary, many primary teachers organize literature circles in which *kids read different books* instead of the same titles. This way, the job of a group member is to give others a taste of the flavor of his or her book, perhaps helping them decide whether they would enjoy reading it.

   • *Children do not take different roles* in these groups. Everyone has basically the same two-part job: to share something of their book, using their log, drawings, or bookmarks as cues, and then to join an open discussion of ideas in the books.

   • When heterogeneous readings are being used, the *group meeting has two phases: sharing and discussion.* Imagine, for example, that each child in a group has been read a different picture book at home the night before. When the literature circle convenes, kids first need to take turns offering some kind of summary, retelling, or read-aloud highlights from their book. Then, discussion can open up in which kids ask one another questions, compare books, and just talk about authors, illustrators, characters, problems, connections, feelings, and ideas.

   • Because books (and attention spans) at this level are short, primary literature circles are typically a *one-meeting event:* a group of kids gathering together on a single occasion to talk about one set of books. The new groups are then formed around another set of readings.

• The *teacher is often present* in primary literature circles. While young children can supervise themselves just fine in well-structured *pair* activities (buddy and partner reading, peer response to writing), some teachers find that more elaborate, larger-group activities like literature circles require more guidance—especially when they are just beginning. If the teacher does elect to attend each group meeting, this has several consequences. First, the rest of the class must be engaged in some other, self-monitored activity (writing workshop, independent reading, etc.), so that the teacher can give her full attention to the circle she's in. As a corollary, making the teacher a group member means that literature circles will meet less often than they would if they were kid-run. Finally, teachers must be very careful not to turn the literature circles into a reading group. The role here is to *facilitate* sharing and discussion, not to teach skills. At other times of the day and week, the teacher has ample opportunities to offer guided instruction, but literature circles are the time for pure, kid-centered book-talk.

Literature Circles in Kindergarten and Early Primary Grades

MARIANNE KROLL AND ANN PAZIOTOPOULOS

PALOS EAST SCHOOL, PALOS HEIGHTS, IL

These two veteran Chicago-area teachers have already published two books on literature circles: *Mark It!* and *Literature Circles: Practical Ideas and Strategies for Responding to Literature*. Both books are especially helpful for adapting the activity to primary-age children. The following selections give the flavor of Ann and Marianne's approach.

Can Literature Circles Be Adapted for the Emergent Reader?

Yes! The emergent reader is a student whose reading ability is in the developmental stage. All the activities involved in literature circles can be adapted for these students. The students can discuss wordless picture books and books with limited print. The students can draw pictures on blank bookmarks to focus on different parts of the story. Activities for these students should emphasize oral language. Emergent readers can benefit cognitively and socially from their participation in literature circles.

Overview: How Do Literature Circles Work?

Initially, the whole class is prepared to read their books using familiar prereading strategies. Next, the students read their books, stopping at appropriate places to reflect on what they have read. Then they select appropriate bookmarks that will guide them during their group discussion. Before the discussion, the students take time to respond in their journals with thoughts and feelings about their books. Books, bookmarks, and journals are brought to the literature circles for discussion.

Step-by-Step Plans

1. Select and discuss bookmarks.

The teacher reads a book orally to the class. Next, the teacher presents a variety of bookmarks, models various ways of selecting appropriate bookmarks, and explains reasons for choosing each bookmark. For example, if the teacher has read *Cinderella* to the class, she might say, "I think that I will choose the bookmark labeled Magic because I can think of several places in the story where the fairy godmother used magic to help Cinderella." The teacher shows the students how to put the bookmarks in the appropriate places in their books so they will be prepared for discussion when they meet in their groups.

2. Respond.

After reading, discussing, and reflecting, students can then respond to their books in a variety of ways. A response journal is an excellent tool that allows all students to freely express their ideas, thoughts, and opinions. The teacher should model the use of the response journal by thinking aloud and then writing responses to a variety of prompts in his/her own journal—just as the students will be doing. After this information has been recorded, the book, bookmarks, and journal are brought to the literature circles for discussion.

3. Form heterogeneous groups.

Students of varying reading abilities are mixed in groups by the teacher. Grouping students heterogeneously offers the following benefits:

- Sharing of reading strategies
- Developing social skills

- Participating in discussions with students of varying abilities, which expands their knowledge base and helps promote self-esteem

4. Students lead groups.

Cooperative learning roles may be used to facilitate the literature circle discussion. Each student is responsible for performing a role in the group. The role of the teacher can be to visit each group and make suggestions, participate, or merely observe. The use of student-led groups allows all groups to meet at the same time. Some suggested roles and responsibilities are:

Journal checker
- checks for completion of journal responses.

Quiet voice monitor
- monitors noise level in group.
- places a red circle in middle of group if noise level becomes unacceptable.

Discussion monitor
- asks each group member to begin their book discussion and encourages all members to participate.
- keeps group members on task.

Observer
- uses a checklist to evaluate the group.
- gives checklist to teacher.

Record keeper
- records the roles for each group member on a class roster.
- records the extension activities for each student on a class roster and passes out the materials needed for the activities. (The use of rosters facilitates the rotation of jobs and activities.)
- keeps all information in folder.

Discussion monitor (teacher, student, or volunteer)
- chooses a student to begin the discussion.
  - student gives a short summary of the book.
  - student talks about his/her bookmarks.
  - student asks for any questions or comments.
- chooses next student to present.

5. Discussions have two stages.

After all students have presented their books, an open discussion begins. Specifically, students look for similarities and differences in their books. Story elements can be compared and contrasted. The students should support their thinking by reading passages from their books. As a product of this activity, students can write a paragraph comparing and contrasting their book with another group member's book.

Literature Circles in Kindergarten and Third Grade

DEBBIE GURVITZ, LYON SCHOOL, GLENVIEW, IL

Literature is the most important component of our curriculum. I read aloud to my students three times a day. Literature is presented for varying purposes, including enjoyment; awareness of story; literacy experiences in reading, writing, and language; awareness of author and illustrator; acquiring information; analyzing and comparing style; and most important, acquiring a disposition to become a lifelong learner.

Last summer I had the opportunity to attend the Walloon Institute, where I gathered additional information about the strategy and use of literature circles in the classroom. Knowing that this concept was originally developed for middle- and upper-level students, I pondered how to implement this strategy in kindergarten. Two questions came to mind as I approached the use of literature circles in the kindergarten classroom. How was I to use this strategy in a developmentally appropriate manner, and how was I to implement this strategy at the emergent-reader level?

Setting the Stage for Literature Circles

The first thing I did was to make sure that my students became familiar with terms that were going to be used in upcoming literature circles. So, in the whole group, we began using the terms illustrator, connector, summarizer, and vocabulary enricher (word wizard) as they came up in discussion following a story. This strategy was not applied during all read-alouds, but only to those I selected or as the terms came up naturally in discussion. In large-group or small-group discussions, or as individuals or pairs, I asked children to respond to a story by creating an illustration, by connecting it to a personal experience, or by summarizing it through dictation. If the children illustrated, connected, or summarized individually or in pairs, we would then compare and contrast illustrations, connections, or summaries in a large-group setting.

Next, I wanted to build kids' familiarity with the terms and processes of cooperative groups. For this practice, we developed an activity around the November 1992 presidential election. The children heard the platforms of three bears running for president. The platforms were presented as read-alouds of *Corduroy*, by Don Freeman, *Good as New*, by Barbara Douglas, and *Jamberry*, by Bruce Degen. The students were randomly placed in three groups. Each group (six students per group) heard one story (platform). The students worked in pairs and were given the following roles: connector (connect to personal experience), illustrator, and summarizer. The children were to present their roles and convince the rest of the classroom to vote for their candidate. All writing was dictated and all roles, whether illustrator, summarizer, or connector, included an illustration by the students. Excellent discussion took place as a result of the use of this strategy. The students did sway some votes in favor of their candidate. All the final writings were placed in a rotating classroom book.

I found this to be a valuable experience, but learned that additional helpers in the room were really necessary to facilitate the process. When we did the election activity, we luckily had the assistance of one parent volunteer and a student teacher. I was at a loss as to how I could move on to real literature circles without having help—more student teachers or parent volunteers—when the solution suddenly appeared.

Literature circles were also being used in several of our third-grade classrooms at Lyon School. As "staff developer," I had the opportunity to observe the implementation of some of these literature circles. While visiting one room, I proposed to the "big kids" that they teach the strategies that they were using in literature circles to my kindergartners.

The third-grade students took their role as "teacher" quite seriously as they conducted their first "inservice" on literature circles. Each kindergarten student was paired with a third grader. The groups consisted of six third-grade students and four kindergarten students. The classes were divided into four groups. Each group was assigned one book written by Mem Fox, our January–February featured author: Group One, *Hattie and the Fox*; Group Two, *Possum Magic*; Group Three, *Koala Lou*; Group Four, *Shoes from Grandpa*.

Three sessions were needed to complete our first round of literature circles. Here's what we did at each meeting:

Session One—The discussion director reintroduced the roles, the literary luminary read the text, and the group members got to know one another.

Session Two—Each group held a literature circle, with each member serving his or her assigned role. The discussion director and literary luminary were facilitators.

Session Three—Small-group and large-group discussions. Evaluation by students and teachers. The goal was to encourage and spark interest for individuals to want to read the books that were presented.

The roles we used were:

Discussion director (third-grade student). Coordinated the activity, redefined roles, and led the discussion.

Literary luminary (third-grade student). Read book to entire group and assisted where needed.

Summarizer (kindergarten student and third-grade student). Kindergarten student dictated summary of story to third-grade student. Third-grade student facilitated discussion and summary.

Reactor (kindergarten student and third-grade student). Kindergarten student dictated reaction and related it to a personal experience. Third-grade student facilitated discussion or summary.

Illustrator (kindergarten student and third-grade student). The kindergarten and third-grade student prepared illustration together and presented illustration to the group.

Word wizard (kindergarten student and third-grade student). Kindergarten student chose three unfamiliar words. Third-grade student used previous knowledge, text, or dictionary to define word. Kindergarten student dictated definition in his/her own words and the students illustrated the word together.

This activity proved very meaningful for both the kindergarten and third-grade children. Students were enthusiastic and energetic when meeting in their groups. They raised good, interesting questions, discussed their reading seriously, and stayed on task most of the time. Students were also able to identify problems they encountered. Some kids thought we had too many sessions, some felt the books were too long, and others admitted that they had been confused at first. The other teachers and I concurred with the students' remarks. We know the next session will be smoother because the students will be familiar with the process, we will use shorter books, we'll have each pair reread the book together before performing their role, and perhaps we will eliminate a couple of roles. If we do this, the groups will be smaller and more manageable. I plan to continue to refine and revise my use of literature circles in the kindergarten classroom.

Exploring Literature Circles in Second Grade

LINDA FULTON, ORLAND CENTER SCHOOL, ORLAND PARK, IL

My second graders' reading program is organized thematically. Usually we spend anywhere from three to six weeks working on a specific theme. I try to incorporate all areas of the curriculum whenever possible. I often use literature circles as a culminating activity to my units, though I feel they can be used effectively at any point in a unit of study. We always read some novels as an entire class, but the literature circles allow children to branch off into smaller interest groups.

My way of using literature circles can best be explained using the diagram on page 116.

When we begin a thematic unit, I choose a core novel to be read by the entire class. In some units, there may be more than one core novel. Each student has his/her own copy of the text. We may spend up to a week reading, discussing, writing, and doing various activities related to the book. Concurrently, I'll be reading aloud to the children from other books related to the same theme. (Some of my units have been organized around a specific author as opposed to a theme.)

After we've finished reading and discussing the core novel(s), I'll have three or four other selections available on the same theme or by the same author. After I give a brief review of each book, the children are able to peruse the books and choose the one they would like to read, thus forming literature circles. While the children read their selection and meet in their literature circles to discuss and react to the book, I act as a facilitator, giving them ideas to think about and allowing them time to write and draw responses in their reading logs. Often, groups culminate their work by developing presentations or performances or artwork about their book for the rest of the class.

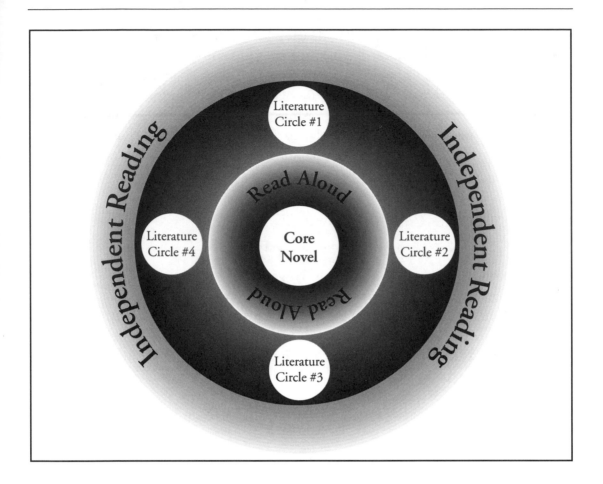

I introduced the first, very simplified form of literature circles late in October. With Halloween just around the corner and everyone's thoughts on ghosts and spooks, I thought the children would enjoy reading books that reflected the "spirit" of the season. These books weren't chosen because they had any exceptional literary qualities, but I knew the subject matter would be appealing.

I collected ten copies each of *Nate the Great and the Halloween Hunt,* by Marjorie Sharmat, *Arthur's Halloween,* by Marc Brown, and *Georgie's Halloween,* by Robert Bright. I gave a short talk about each book and showed a few illustrations from each. Then I asked the children to think about which one they would most like to read. I gave everyone a sheet of paper containing a list of the books, and each child was told to rate them one, two, or three, with one being their first choice. The children were organized into three literature circles according to their selection. All the children were able to read either their first or second choice.

During the next class session, I passed out the books. The children seemed very excited about reading the books. I gave them the option of reading independently, reading with a partner who shared the same book, or joining with all of the students who shared the same book to read as a group. Most of the students opted to read with a partner, but the children reading *Arthur's Halloween* sat in a circle and read the book together. They stayed on task and took turns with the reading. One person took charge of the group and everyone else was content to follow along. They read page by page, around the circle, and everyone had an opportunity to read.

Some children finished reading sooner than others. When everyone had finished reading, we met together as a class, and I told the children to take out their reading logs. Our reading logs are spiral notebooks in which the children can respond freely to their reading. The reading logs served as a springboard to the next day's book discussions. I asked the children to write a few sentences in their logs telling about their favorite part of the book and why they had chosen it as their favorite. Then I gave them a separate piece of paper on which to illustrate their selection.

The next day, I explained that the children would be meeting in literature circles to discuss their books. They were to bring their reading logs and illustrations to the group discussion and take turns telling about their favorite parts and sharing their illustrations. Because this was their first experience with literature circles, I felt more comfortable having them use their logs as a starting point for their discussions. I didn't want to discourage their conversations from taking other directions, but at least I knew they had somewhere to begin. I told them I would be walking around the room, listening to their discussions and looking for people who showed me they remembered our rules about working cooperatively.

As I walked from group to group, I stopped to listen to parts of the discussions. I was pleased that some of the children were beginning to interact with each other by asking questions about illustrations and making comments like, "That was my favorite part too." Two of the groups worked extremely well. A third group needed some encouragement from me. Though this group contained several good readers, they were still arguing about who was going to go first. It seemed there were too many leaders in the group. I got them started by asking a few questions and sharing my feelings about the book. They started to react to some of my comments, and soon the discussion began to roll.

I kept moving around the room, but paid particular attention to the group that had had the most difficulty getting started. I noticed that after one person finished speaking, hands would shoot into the air, and the speaker would choose the next person to talk. I don't know if this procedure stifled conversation, but it kept order in the group. They are familiar with this procedure in a large-group or class discussion, and I often let one student call on the next rather than calling on individuals myself.

After a period of about twenty minutes, we gathered together as a class. I wanted to get feedback about the group activities. I was very curious about what they especially liked or disliked about the day's activities. Many of the children said they liked choosing their own books and that it was fun to meet in groups without the teacher. A few students were quick to point a finger at members in their groups who were not behaving. I didn't want this to become a tattling session and quickly turned the conversation around by asking the children to tell me about the things that make a group function successfully. We reviewed the rules of cooperative learning, which we had discussed earlier in the year.

It seemed that the children enjoyed these initial book discussions, and they asked if they could trade books and do it again. I told them that all three books would be available for independent reading, but we wouldn't be forming literature circles again using these books. I informed them of my plan to try literature circles again at the conclusion of our next reading unit, which focused on mysteries. The response from the children was a resounding yes.

Although I was pleased with the way the children responded to our first experience with literature circles, I knew that eventually I wanted the discussions to be more student driven. I wanted to see more interaction in the groups. During the next several weeks I started to demonstrate questioning techniques that would give the children greater opportunities to discuss literature and share their feelings. I wanted to get away from the literal types of questions that involved selecting a "right" answer. The children were encouraged to do more predicting and hypothesizing about their reading. They were also encouraged to share their own feelings and personal stories. Literature becomes so much more meaningful when we connect it to our own lives and experiences.

We did several more cycles of literature circles throughout the year, and whether it was with mysteries, fairy tales, or any other unit, everyone enjoyed the literature circles.

I was particularly interested in the responses I received from the children who have reading difficulties. During individual interviews with some of these students, they indicated that they liked working in literature circles better than when we discussed books as an entire class. Again, a popular reason was the opportunity to choose their own books. Another reason was that it was more fun to work with friends. I think that the smaller group size was less intimidating to these children, and because the groups were not organized according to achievement, they felt equal to their peers.

Everyone came to their literature circle meetings prepared to share in the conversation. Nobody was caught off guard. Each child had the opportunity to join in the discussion whenever he or she felt inclined. The less proficient readers seemed to participate with as much confidence as the other students. They didn't seem to get lost like they often do in a large group.

There are many components that have contributed to the overall effectiveness of my reading program, but the addition of literature circles added a new dimension that produced a lot of smiles and good feelings. I plan to continue to incorporate literature circles into my reading program. My research and experience have led me to believe that there isn't one right way to conduct literature circles, and so I will continue to experiment with a variety of ideas and techniques.

Literature Circles in Primary Special Education

JUDITH HECHLER, SOUTH SCHOOL, DES PLAINES, IL

I teach a primary self-contained special education class for students with learning disabilities. Most of the children in my class are two years below grade level in reading decoding, but are quite adept at understanding what they hear. They also have quite strong verbal abilities, so discussions are many and animated. The physical act of writing is difficult for most, and needless to say, their writing skills are at the same level as their reading decoding.

For our first attempt with literature circles we read *Sarah, Plain and*

Tall, by Patricia MacLachlan. Rather than putting students in groups with each student having an assigned role, the whole class worked on each role, one after the other, for each chapter. All of us did one job at a time. After that job was completed, we moved on to the next

For instance, the first job for the class was to be the illustrator. This particular book had no illustrations, so I presented the idea that they could draw pictures to go along with the chapter we had just completed. They were able to make their own choice of what to draw from the reading. When all the drawings were completed, we glued them on a large piece of butcher paper so that it resembled a story quilt. We hung the chapter illustrations along the wall as we completed each chapter. At the end of the book, we had quite a collection of drawings, but the best part was that every student could go to the chapter illustrations and retell the events from that chapter.

When we took on the discussion director role, I would often ask questions geared to prompt the students to put themselves in the position of one of the characters. This discussion format put the students at ease and they in turn asked questions of me and each other along the lines of, Why do you think . . .? What would you have done about . . .? How did you feel when . . .?

We all acted as vocabulary enrichers whenever we came upon an unfamiliar word. Everyone knew it was acceptable to interrupt (politely, of course) the reading in order to ask what a word meant. We would also discuss what other word could have been used in its place.

The role of passage master became a springboard for writing in our journals. We would collectively discuss the parts we liked best and why. I would list these on the board, and then we all wrote our contribution in our journal, with an explanation of why we chose it.

A later adaptation I used was to assign the students to one of four task groups. Each group then took turns being discussion director, illustrator, vocabulary enricher, and passage master. Our teaching assistant monitored two groups, while I monitored the other two. This way of grouping worked well with either chapter books or picture books.

The four roles used in literature circles actively involve the children in the literature, rather than permit them to be passive listeners/daydreamers. I was continually surprised when they related incidents from *Sarah, Plain and Tall* to other stories, and even to television programs, months after we had finished reading it.

Nonfiction and Fiction Literature Circles in Third Grade

CHERYL FOERTSCH, CENTENNIAL SCHOOL, ORLAND PARK, IL

I was originally turned on to the idea of literature circles by listening to my colleague Regina Knapp in a staff development course on whole language. She explained how literature circles worked in her classroom. They made so much sense. She described children actively involved in a piece of reading in a natural way. Later on in the year, another presenter came to our school for an institute day. He brought more examples of literature circles with him, sharing role sheets already developed by other teachers. With the samples to go on, I felt ready to give it a try. I decided to adapt the job sheets for the two settings in which I wanted to try literature circles: fiction and nonfiction.

Nonfiction Literature Circles

The first thing I needed to do was to familiarize the students with the various job sheets. I decided that the best way to do this was to let them try each job with a different assignment. I broke the students into partner groups. I chose to use biographies for this initial exposure to the various jobs, since we had at least two copies per title, they were short, and biography fit well with the core piece I wanted to use for the "real" literature circles, *What's the Big Idea, Ben Franklin?* by Jean Fritz.

Each partner group chose the title they wanted to read first. They both read the book and filled out the same job sheet. They got together to discuss the book, using the job sheet as a guide for their discussion. Then they chose their next title. This time they had to choose a different job sheet to fill out. This continued until they had read five different titles, filling out each of the five different job sheets: director, connector, illustrator, story highlighter, and word wizard.

The biography unit was a great success. The students were very proud to have read five different titles. From here we went into our core novel for the unit, *What's the Big Idea, Ben Franklin?* This time I split the children into groups of five (one group had to be six). This way each job could be represented in the group.

As I read the novel again to prepare for the unit, I decided on the logical cutoff points, so that the story could be read in five different sessions. Each night the children were to read the assigned pages from the story and fill out the job sheet they had chosen for that particular assignment.

Since each group member was to choose a different job, they were ensuring a more well-rounded discussion when they came to their literature circle.

When it was time for reading the next day, I first asked for volunteers to read the section of text aloud, in order to familiarize everyone with the reading about to be discussed. From here the students broke into their various literature circle groups and began the discussion. The director was to lead the discussion and decide the order in which the different jobs would be shared.

I took the opportunity to sit in on one group per day and participate with that group. I was utterly amazed at the level of discussion for each group. While I needed to clarify some of the roles and how they were to share their information, the students were always prepared. After each discussion session, the students filled out an evaluation for that day's meeting. Each time, I truly felt that the kids took the evaluation seriously and really reflected on what worked and what didn't. Overall, I was very happy with these nonfiction literature circles, and so were the students.

Fiction Literature Circles

My first attempt at using literature circles with fiction was in a unit on tall tales. We started the unit by reading a core title together as a whole group—*Paul Bunyan,* by Steven Kellogg. As we read, laughed about, and discussed the book, the children became aware of the "tall tale" genre.

After we finished the core title, I broke the students into groups of five (two groups were six). I had acquired ten copies each of three separate titles: *Pecos Bill,* by Steven Kellogg, *Johnny Appleseed,* by Steven Kellogg, and *John Henry,* by Ezra Jack Keats. The groups were to rotate among the three titles, each time choosing a different role sheet to complete. That way, each student completed three of the five job sheets, although everyone was exposed to all the jobs during discussion, since no two people from the five-person groups were to choose the same job.

To finish the unit, the students brainstormed how they might do a project on one of the titles. They worked together in their groups on completing the projects. Among those chosen were shadow boxes, puppets, posters, maps, and clay models. This unit was also very successful. The students liked having to make their own choices and decisions. The quality of their reading, their attitudes in class, and their projects were wonderful.

Literature Circles in Fourth-Grade Social Studies

PAT GARDNER, CENTENNIAL SCHOOL, ORLAND PARK, IL

I have explored using literature circles with some social studies units over the last couple of years. Using this strategy, the study of remote cultures changed from a boring activity to one of personal identification for the children. Before, it often took forever to cover the readings of the first three primary cultures in social studies, and I could feel myself struggling with the lessons. These units were so far removed from our own culture that children could not and/or would not relate and were bored. I had been using literature circles (with literature, of course) and suddenly one day I had a vision. Why not try literature circles with our study of cultures?

As I began to work through this inspiration, the idea of stacking other strategies with literature circles began to emerge. At the beginning of the cultural study, the children liked the idea of different groups working on different cultures. They began to identify with each group, calling themselves by the native names of the particular group.

The first step involved jigsawing the three cultures. We studied three cultures using six groups. Each child in the group was responsible for certain passages and/or selections. I might say this was jigsawing within jigsawing. Upon completion of their study, the groups reported by presenting to the whole class.

Role assignment within the groups changed somewhat from the original literature circle roles, utilizing five specific tasks. The illustrator was still supposed to draw and explain a selected passage's main idea. The word finder was to select words that could be compared or contrasted with our society. A Venn diagram was used for this. For example, the different roles of men and women, artifacts used, and the like could be compared and contrasted. The picture person was to choose illustrations, pictures, and maps to show to the class and to encourage discussion about them. The spider was to make a semantic web and then explain the main ideas of the story. The question asker (we called this role the lawyer) presented tough questions, using "why?" to provoke discussions. This final task was presented after all previous information was given.

Motivation grew as each child became more invested. I needed to serve as facilitator only until the groups began to understand their specific roles and work cooperatively. When there were not enough children in a group, some of the roles were combined. Children for the most part did not mind having two jobs. It was especially interesting to note the similarities and differences in the way the groups who studied the same cultures presented their information to the class.

Fourth-Grade Circles of Cooperative Creativity

DEBRA O'CONNOR, CENTENNIAL SCHOOL, ORLAND PARK, IL

I first learned of literature circles last year in a whole language class offered by my district. This strategy stressed collaboration and teamwork, which seemed well suited to my teaching style. I was eager to give it a shot. So I tried literature circles in various curricular situations (e.g., an author study of Beverly Cleary), but found that my kids hadn't had enough modeling of or practice in cooperative grouping behaviors earlier in the year. Too much time was being spent settling disputes between students within groups. I wanted to be a facilitator of literature circles, not a referee!

This year I tried something different. I began the year with many social skills lessons about group behavior (e.g., team building, developing a sense of belonging, encouraging others, quiet voices). I did this with the hope of getting as much as possible out of the literature circle strategy without the behavior problems I'd previously experienced. Now, I have found that preparation time spent in the first two weeks of school has helped enormously in both cooperative group work and classroom management in general.

After establishing an understanding of cooperation, we dove headfirst into *The Witch of Fourth Street,* by Myron Levoy. This book is an interesting collection of eight short stories about immigrants and integrates well with our social studies unit on immigration. It is part of the fourth-grade curriculum, but contains some concepts that are difficult for some students to understand. It seemed a reasonable choice to break into smaller sections (i.e., jigsaw) to ease comprehension and discussion.

I introduced the concept of literature circles by relating it to other cooperative grouping we had experienced in class. We discussed the idea of each student having a role to do in a literature circle. The other fourth-grade teachers and I had worked on some job titles and descriptions that we felt would be appropriate for our students when using this strategy. I proceeded to give the children a summary of four roles and the tasks they would be expected to perform in each. We discussed the job descriptions. Each child was then given a role at random. The role was to be completed on a sheet that contained detailed instructions for that role. I used these worksheet guides with the hope that with more practice they would be able to use their reading journals to complete literature circle tasks. The students were asked to keep their role in mind while we read the first story aloud together. They were then given time to complete their task. Upon completion, they met with other students who had the same role. They discussed their findings with one another and were encouraged to add or delete anything from their work that was appropriate. We then met as an entire group to discuss the results. This exercise was to give some experience to each child and to expose everyone to the various roles.

The children were then randomly broken into groups of four (six groups total). Each student in a group was given a different role to perform. They were then asked to form a circle somewhere in the room, and read the last story in the book to each other. They were given time to complete their tasks and to discuss. We then came together as a class and talked about what had gone well and the questions that had surfaced.

Next, each group chose a different story in the book. Each student also chose a different role to perform for their circle. The students were responsible for reading the story, completing the roles, conducting their own small-group discussion, and finally presenting their story to the class. They worked together well (that's not to say that some "whistle blowing" wasn't necessary, but very few "fouls" occurred). Each group was able to choose how they would present their story: a puppet show, readers theater with props, a play, etc. They were evaluated on how well they presented the main idea and the plot of their story to the rest of the class, and how well suited the presentation was to their story (i.e., readers theater was appropriate if the story contained enough dialogue to make it interesting). After each presentation, the rest of the class wrote a summary of what they thought the story was about. The presenting groups were given the summaries and asked to evaluate how well the class understood the plot and main idea of their story. They were then asked to write about their part in the presentation and to evaluate themselves and their group. This process was time-consuming, but less lengthy and more interesting than having each child read and try to comprehend all the stories in this somewhat tedious collection.

I enjoy using literature circles in this way. It allows me to facilitate the students' learning, while they enjoy the creativity and freedom of choice this strategy allows. Literature circles take much preplanning, practice, and modeling, but I find them to be a valuable activity for every player on the team.

Exploration Circles in Fifth Grade

JUDITH ALFORD, MAPLEWOOD SCHOOL, CARY, IL

In 1991, I read an article by Marianne Flanagan, "Starting Literature Circles in the Fifth Grade." At the same time, I was exploring the idea of giving my kids more choices in the classroom and the relationship of choices to student self-esteem.

From the beginning of the year, my students had been making some choices about bulletin board displays, seating arrangements, and classroom tasks. By the time we got to choosing topics to study and books to read, a lot of their earlier insecurities, like constantly checking with me to see whether their choices were okay, had disappeared. I believe part of that "checking in" was testing me to see if I was really going to let them choose. It was not always easy to keep my fingers out, especially when the bulletin boards all turned black and stayed that way the whole year. But the kids loved it. I wanted other colors but stayed true to my promise that they could choose.

To allow for the greatest amount of freedom and student choice, I had worked out a special half-hour block of time in which groups of students could work on whatever they chose without formal curriculum restraints. This also gave me an opportunity to work with the children for part of the day without having to grade them. I renamed this activity exploration circles instead of literature circles. The students brainstormed topics they wished to know more about and then formed groups around their common interests. Mostly, I stayed out of their group formation process.

In this format, specific task responsibilities evolved out of the groups themselves. Kids decided on what materials to use, who would write, who was to gather pictures for the final project or presentation. We brainstormed a list of ways to handle the reading involved, including the group's assigning the pages or different kids' reading different books on behalf of the group. During the process they set dates for completing readings, projects, or other tasks. They learned to adjust the dates according to their group members' progress and the progress of the rest of the class. Whole-class progress meetings were held every couple of days.

Three Cycles of Exploration Circles

We did three kinds of exploration circles, and each time students used a different method to choose their partners. During the first cycle the entire class brainstormed topics of interest. The topics were written down and Xeroxed. Each student then prioritized five interesting topics by numbering from one to five, one being the most interesting. The students were grouped by their number-one choice. If there was no one else interested in a given topic, the student could change topics or choose to work alone. Only three students chose to work alone.

Another opportunity to change topics was provided if the group had difficulty finding information in our school learning center or the public library or could not find an expert who could supply them with additional information. Two boys, Timbo and Air J., decided to combine their topics of steam engines and diesel engines into a report on railroads. Students could also change their topic after one week if it turned out to be not so desirable or, in their words, "boring." After one week, they had to have arrived at a topic that they would stick with and ultimately present to the class.

One group of boys decided to find out about cars. They began cutting out and collecting over a hundred pictures of cars from magazines, newspapers, and calendars. They glued them into a huge, butcher-paper collage. This was going to be their finished project. When they went before the class, the students pressed them for what they had learned and why they did the collage. The class realized that this group had not done enough on their topic, and told them so.

Then the boys dug out some books about car engines and made a second poster about automobile engines. The boys decided they had made the collage because they liked the way the cars looked. During their conversation they decided to survey the rest of the class concerning their favorite cars. The boys then numbered each picture in the original collage with a permanent marker and developed a graph on butcher paper so the class could record their choices.

During their second presentation, the boys demonstrated they had learned that most of the class liked sports cars. They had also learned that constructing a graph based on a field of one hundred choices was not as easy as it looked, but they had been able to measure the paper and divide it to record the information. When the boys later wrote in their journals about their group's process, they mentioned they were glad I didn't tell them what they had to learn about cars and that I didn't yell at them about not working enough the first time around. They enjoyed making choices about their project and liked being treated as if they had a brain to make decisions.

Our second cycle of exploration circles was more like traditional literature circles. I provided some good novels for them to choose from. I ordered five copies of various paperbacks and did a brief book review about each. The books were *A Gathering of Days,* by Jean Blos, *Indian Chiefs,* by Russell Freeman, *Six Months to Live,* by Lurlene McDaniel, *Let the Circle Be Unbroken,* by Mildred Taylor, *Faithful Friend,* by Beatrice Siegel, and *The Sign of the Beaver,* by Elizabeth Speare. After I presented the book reviews, the students were given a ballot listing the names of the books. They numbered the selections from one to six according to preference. Group size was limited to five because I only had five copies of each book. All the students either received their first or second choice.

Groups decided how they would handle the reading. The choices were to read silently during class and at home the number of pages decided by the group; to read the book together in a group during class; or to appoint someone who would read the book to the group. While the group reading *Indian Chiefs* began reading the book together, the different reading abilities soon became a frustration to both the more able and the slower readers. Then they decided to assign pages, determine when the reading should be done, and then discuss the pages as a group. The rest of the groups decided from the beginning to assign pages and discuss the readings in class on a given date. Reading the pages independently appeared to be a good face-saving device for the less swift readers. Parents were encouraged to help with the reading process. The faster readers were able to read ahead and enjoy the book at their own pace, too.

In the third cycle, kids had an even more open choice. I invited students to brainstorm any kind of project they wished to do. The students discussed what they wanted to do, categorized the ideas into three options—free choice, having me read a book to the whole class, or working together in book-buddy teams—and then rated these options as their first, second, or third choice. The kids decided that "free choice" was what they wanted to do. (The few students that still wanted me to read to them were allowed the option of doing that while the rest of the class worked on their projects.)

Ice Man and Short Stuff chose to study humor. Blue Eyes, Heavenly Joy, and Boomer decided to do a play. The two groups then joined to do a humorous play. This group built their own sets, collected props, and rehearsed on their own time. Combining the two groups allowed them to have enough participants to enact the characters and pursue humor, too.

Several students chose to read another paperback and discuss it with a friend. It was exciting to see four students who at the beginning of the year had expressed hatred for reading choose this option. They selected books at their comfort level, and only asked my assistance in gathering materials to complete their final project.

Looking Back on Exploration Circles

Problems: To prevent students from always choosing the same friends to work with, the topic selections and book selections were done by secret ballot, with no opportunity to discuss ideas at recess. I feel this is justified, since at other times of the day, kids have plenty of opportunities to work with their friends. (And sometimes I do select groups keeping in mind abilities, personalities, etc.)

Benefits: The greatest benefits are that the majority of students eagerly participate in group and class discussions, they are empowered by their choices, they stretch their learning beyond teacher expectations, they are excited about what they are doing, and the whole process gives room for individuals to be individuals. Kids love not only jigsawing what they are reading in literature circles, but sharing what they are reading for book reports or other projects. They love suggesting what the class might do next and suggesting books for the teacher and others to read.

Feelings: At first I had worries of, Am I doing a good job? What should a teacher do here? But once I realized it was okay for a student to say no to a suggestion from me, and once I started getting used to the feeling I wasn't needed, the students kept me more than busy. They wanted me to copy pages, gather materials, schedule learning center times, check out filmstrips, and read and respond to journal entries. I was simply a facilitator, offering open-ended questions to help students solve their own problems or find their own answers to their questions. I didn't want them to do it any other way.

Much like the writing process, literature/exploration circles are a process of moving from dependence to independence. But each class and year is different. It depends on the personalities of the children and teacher, the expectations, and the exposure to choice. It appeared the more choices I gave most students, the more willing they were to give others choices as well.

Fifth-Grade Literature Circles, Centennial-Style

JAYNE O'NEILL, CENTENNIAL SCHOOL, ORLAND PARK, IL

Preparing students to work in literature circles has proven to be critical for their success in our fifth-grade classrooms. We always start using literature circles with the students all reading the same short story. Then we move on to reading the same novel before we try literature circles with six or seven different books. We feel this prepares the students for more advanced literature circles.

We begin work with literature circles by familiarizing students with the various roles and modeling them carefully. This training is done using a short story over approximately five days. Each day the teacher asks the class to read a short segment of the story and models one literature circle role. This seems to work best by using a transparency of the role sheet on the overhead projector, and giving each student his or her own copy to complete. Ideas are discussed and added to the individual student's sheet. The next day, the same procedure is followed: the class reads another segment of the short story, the teacher models a different role, and the students complete a copy of the role sheet. This process continues until all the roles have been explained and the students are ready to try them on their own.

We give the students a book choice sheet if we are using more than one novel. We do our best to honor kids' preferences and meet their needs. Once the students are in their literature circles, the reading can be done however they wish—silently, with a buddy, one by one in the group, the teacher reading aloud to the whole class, etc.—depending on whether the students are all reading the same novel or different novels. Sometimes we assign how the students will read that day.

When it is time to assign the roles, we always record on a class list ahead of time the roles each student will be given. This also helps in case there is a substitute in the classroom. The students are not allowed to complain or ask for a different role, because they know they will be assigned all the roles eventually.

We designed new role sheets because we found the generic ones too difficult to use. We shortened the directions and made them more specific. We added lines for neatness and redesigned the format so all the roles are consistent. At the top of each role sheet it states it is worth twenty-five points. We give exact points, so the students know ahead of time how they will be evaluated. We also combined the illustrator and connector into one role, since we feel these two roles involve less work than the others. Therefore, our literature circles are made up of four students instead of five. We find an even number of students works better than an odd number.

If it is not possible to have four students in a group, we'll let it grow to five. Then the roles of illustrator and connector are separated, but the point value does not change—they're worth twenty-five points together. When students are absent we assign them the role of illustrator/connector, which they can accomplish at home. On the following day the literature circle discussion can still flow freely.

Usually we assign days by which chapters or pages must be read and an LC role completed. We meet approximately every other day in literature circles. This gives the students time to complete their tasks. The reading and roles are started in class and completed at home. On the assigned day the literature circles get together to discuss their roles and what they've read. In between, we can teach a skill or do an activity we have designed. This gives us a little more input than if the students are left totally on their own during the entire novel.

Discussion Groups

When the students are in their literature circles, we walk around and monitor them. We move between groups and sit with them, listening to their discussions. Once in a while we will ask a question, make a comment or a suggestion, or simply make sure the students are on task. We do allow the student discussion directors to run the discussion. We give the literature circles fifteen to twenty minutes total to discuss their roles. This gives each student approximately five minutes, give or take, since some of the roles are more involved than others.

We do not allot an entire reading class to discussion. Once we halt a discussion, we then assign the next required reading. As students begin reading, we walk around and make sure kids know their new roles. Assigning the reading works best if the students are all reading the same novel, because then we can assign chapters and pace the students. This enables us to monitor the students' progress better and bring the class back together as a whole for discussion and questions. When different novels are being read, it may be more beneficial to assign pages instead of chapters.

CHAPTER SEVEN

• • • • • • • • •

Teachers' Applications: Middle School Through College

Although well-planned and well-executed collaboration can be wonderful for everyone involved, we all know how frustrating a sloppily planned and carried-out collaborative activity can be. Good collaboration takes the careful planning and monitoring of a skillful teacher.

> —*Marline Pearson, Madison Area Technical College*

IT CAN seem pretty daunting to work literature circles into a secondary or college teaching schedule. Not only is the departmentalized structure a deterrent, but the typically overstuffed, mandated curriculum makes teachers feel like there just isn't time for anything extra or new. But these five teachers have found a variety of ways to bring literature circles to their adolescent and young adult students.

Literature Circles in Middle School

SHARON WEINER, BAKER DEMONSTRATION SCHOOL, EVANSTON, IL

Last year, I introduced literature circles to my seventh-grade class. I was exploring various ways of improving the quality of kids' literature discussions, in terms of both investment and insight. Admittedly, I was skeptical about the ability of kids to direct their own discussions with enough depth. However, too many kids were unwilling to trust their own responses—they far too often wanted to know what the "official" interpretation of an event or character was or what I (the allegedly infallible teacher) thought the story "meant." I knew I needed to provide a structure to help kids develop and

133

133

trust their own readings. So I briefed them with some background on *Beowulf,* and we jumped in.

On the first day, I gave kids a set of lit circle role sheets. They discussed and debated the roles, and worked in single-task teams (all the passage masters together, all discussion directors together, etc.), developing their responses to the first part of the tale, "The Story of Grendel." They discussed the similarities and differences in their responses to the same task. (The hard part here was convincing some kids to trust their own responses rather than look to the others.) I put same-task kids together so they would have confidence in the basic focus of their role, and so they could help one another fill out the preparation sheet. I think this gave them the confidence to begin.

The second day, the kids discussed "Grendel" in literature circles, with each member of a circle taking a different role. Even with just their previous day's preparation, I was amazed at the depth of their discussions. At the end of the day they decided to stay in their literature circles but to switch tasks for the second part of the tale, "Grendel's Mother."

On the third day, for the "Grendel's Mother" discussion, the kids came into class and immediately got into their circles and began their discussion. This was especially striking because I was late to class. I expected to walk into chaos. Instead I found (as I walked in fully six or seven minutes late) a smoothly operating class—four literature circles in earnest discussion. I have never seen a model for discussion that was so intuitive to kids, and so well liked.

I have played with the model in several ways. Sometimes, we decide to have a researcher role. This individual finds and reports on interesting background information about an author or a topic, with support from the librarians and me. The research topic is up to the researchers, not me, and is therefore almost guaranteed to be of interest to the group. The one big rule is that the researcher must always clearly tie his or her information with details from the reading. The kids are often extremely insightful and original in their research topics. For example, one eighth-grade researcher brought in art books by concentration camp victims for a group reading of Elie Weisel's *Night.* I think this is a great way to individualize the teaching of research skills, and kids seem to love this role.

Literature circles are also a natural structure for novel or short story units that involve student choice. I put out more sets of novels or stories (sometimes kids bring in sets of stories) than there are possible groups in a class. Kids then arrange themselves by their interest in reading a particular story (but there must be complete groups). After reading the story at home and preparing for the discussion, they discuss the story in their literature circle. At the end of each discussion, kids choose their next story to be read in re-formed groups.

I have also organized circles around read-alouds. The kids are first organized into literature circles and choose tasks. Then I like to read (or have kids read) the selection twice—once for overall listening and pleasure, and once again for analysis. The second time, kids listen for their specific task—passage picking, illustrating, etc. This works well, because the kids focus on their jobs as they listen. They then discuss the reading in literature circles, with a copy of the selection for reference. This really helps kids see how listening for specific purposes alters the listening process, and they have become increasingly better listeners.

Another variation on the model is based on reading workshop activities. As students read books they have individually chosen, they respond at various times in their reading journal. Occasionally, I ask them to respond in the manner of the roles they now know so well—passage master, discussion director, summarizer, or vocabularian. Then I ask kids to share what they have written, in small groups or (on occasion) with the group as a whole. I think this has two benefits. It is, in a way, an approach to book-talks—to exposing the whole class to books that individuals are reading. This approach also offers kids who are reading the same or related books opportunities for discussion—something that often seems missing in reading workshops. As an additional benefit, kids are now much more aware of vocabulary than when they read purely independently.

To sum up, my students really love literature circles. They like the comfort of the structure, but also the flexibility of the multiple roles. They see that this one structure can be applied to multiple tasks—small-group reading, read-alouds, independent reading. They learn that understanding comes from more than one direction. Most important, they learn to trust themselves and respect one another as discussers and analysts. They bring up what is important to them, and in doing so seem to connect more deeply with the reading. I enjoy and value this approach to reading, but far more important, so do my students.

Can Freshman Fundamentals Do Literature Circles?

SUZY RUDER, CARL SANDBURG HIGH SCHOOL, ORLAND PARK, IL

I teach English in a large suburban high school where, since I am a reading specialist, most of my classes are remedial in nature. In my Freshman Fundamental classes (reading level 3.0–6.0) I have tried to involve the students in their learning by using literature circles. These classes are made up of the "D" (for disabled) group: BD, LD, ADD, ED, unidentified Ds, etc. Very few "regular ed" students are enrolled. Last year a revolving door seemed to have been placed in the room, too. We were never quite sure who was rolling in or out: a total of forty-one students rotated through the course. Quite an atmosphere in which to do quality and continuous work! I was willing to give this group a chance at sitting in groups of four or five and expressing their ideas about the novel *Island Keeper,* by Harry Mazer.

To begin the training, I decided on four roles: word wizard, literary luminary, discussion director, and creative connector. Creative connector was a role that I devised because students so often comment, Why are we doing this . . . what does this have to do with *me*? The role of the creative connector is twofold. First of all, this student must make a personal connection to an idea in the chapter. Secondly, he or she must pose questions that will prompt each member of the literature circle to make some sort of personal connection. Frequent questions are: Have you ever felt . . .? Can you think of a time when you did something similar to the actions of the main character in this chapter? This role generated the most excitement. Students chattered away all the while doing a mental comparison/contrast with the text. I threw out the old role of "narc," oops, process checker, because it seemed to make that person a tattletale—someone working against the group. That person also felt no vested interest in the material—just in reporting on the "bad guys."

After deciding the roles, I took into account that many of my students were visual learners, so I redesigned the basic forms by using computer clip-art designs depicting the activity at the top of each sheet. For example, the discussion director shows a conductor directing an orchestra. I also changed the language to a more informal style—hoping to appeal to students.

I felt that I needed to sell this idea to this unique group of students, and who could better help me than my friend Calvin from "Calvin and

Hobbes," the comic strip? I placed the students into four large groups: WW, LL, DD, and CC. For example, all word wizards were in one group. They discussed their role, read the full-page comic "story" and prepared their sheets together. Next we jigsawed, making groups of four or five with each different role being represented. The discussion directors in each group took over and they "roled" (I couldn't resist!) on. The students especially liked Calvin's vocabulary—I made sure I'd selected a strip that included one of his "space" words, which couldn't be found in a dictionary. Of course, WWs were in their glory as they made their group dig through the context to come up with a viable meaning. There were millions of questions—but that sure beat the poking, put-downs, and usual antics. When students asked me about a role, I turned them toward another person with the same role who could probably explain it better than I could.

Then we tackled a whole novel. As we worked with *Island Keeper,* I still did give chapter quizzes. But now all quizzes included open-ended questions similar to those on the lit circle role sheets, questions that asked students to connect, to draw, etc. Some quizzes simply asked the student to make up three good questions and answer them. No true-false or multiple-guess testing occurred. When I would suggest that we didn't need a quiz after a particular chapter, they balked—they wanted to show what they had learned.

Some days I allowed the group to take the quiz en masse, on others the quiz was an individual effort, and on still others the quiz grade was the average of the group. I assigned groups (I had to keep some of them separated!) and roles for four chapters at a time, then I would mix them up for the next four chapters. I posted charts in advance so a suspended student could attempt to stay abreast. I made my chronic truants and suspendees the fifth role in the group—repeating Student A—so no one felt excluded. The chart follows:

| | Chapter | | | |
	1	2	3	4
Student A	LL	DD	CC	WW
Student B	WW	LL	DD	CC
Student C	CC	WW	LL	DD
Student D	DD	CC	WW	LL
Student E	LL	DD	CC	WW

Each chapter took about two days. For the first few chapters, I had all of the DDs, etc., meet together before jigsawing back into the above chart.

Was the class perfect? Not by a long stretch. However, I hoped that I was giving them the message that I trusted their willingness to work in groups and that I respected their ability to extract important concepts from a text. It was a risk worth taking because they didn't want to do this on their own. I'm sure we had a lot better chance of doing our work this way than if I had used a traditional method. One particular student who all year long had silently refused to involve himself in sustained silent reading became so involved that he designed a "final project" for the book. He crossed over the line into literacy. Was it literature circles, Harry Mazer's heroine Cleo, or just the right moment?

I also continue to use literature circles in my "academic" classes. This year in sophomore literature we used them successfully with *To Kill a Mockingbird.* Students seem drawn to comparing their own lives with Scout, Jem, and Dill. I didn't grade the daily role sheets—good golly, I'm not a fool! I did check to see if each circle had all participants prepared. I simply circulated with a "piggy" rubber stamp to show the sheet was completed according to schedule. No one quite knew what the "piggies" meant—adding a little mystery to the moment. At the end of the book, we counted our piggies and received some points for completion. I thought I should revise the style of the sheets since they might be considered a little young—but the sophomores, juniors, and even senior Brit Lit students thought they were *fun*—the "f" word we're always looking for.

High School Advanced Placement and Chapter I

MARIA WARD, GLENBARD EAST HIGH SCHOOL, LOMBARD, IL

Glenbard East High School is one of four schools in District 87, a middle-class system of approximately 7,500 students. The school enrollment is around 1,800 students, of whom 23 percent are minorities. I am the English department chairperson in this building, and I teach two classes: an advanced placement senior English class (British literature, primarily) and a study skills class for students who are considered "at risk." I have used literature circles with both groups but will begin my account with what I did with my AP class.

Advanced Placement Senior English

I began using literature circles because I wanted to encourage close reading and a student-centered learning environment. I had begun fostering the close reading on the first day of class when I told students they would need to keep a reading log all year. I explained what I meant by a reading log, gave them some examples, and told them I would collect them about every two weeks. They would earn five points per page for anything beyond the minimum. After the first collection of mostly inadequate reading logs, I shared a few exemplary logs and told them in a stern but loving tone of voice what I expected for the next go-round. The following collection date brought a wealth of interesting observations, reflections, and questions about what the students were reading, and I knew the logs would greatly enhance the literature circles I would launch with *The Canterbury Tales.*

I began using literature circles with "The Knight's Tale." We had already read and discussed the "Prologue" and were ready to begin the first tales. On the day the tale was due, I told students we were going to prepare for small-group discussion by having them be responsible for different roles in the discussion. I had already determined who I wanted to serve in each role—discussion director, literary luminary, and vocabulary enricher. (I would ultimately include the capable connector role after we read several tales.) As much as possible, I wanted to ensure the success of literature circles, so I gave the strongest students the role of discussion director. In this particular section of AP, most of the students are quite strong, however, so I knew that the other roles would not really suffer. I explained each role to the students, giving them examples of the kinds of things they should be developing and/or looking for before I gave them their role sheets. I then told students to get into role-alike groups to prepare for the discussion they would have later in the period when they broke into groups, one of each role in a group.

Students moved quickly to their groups and I proceeded to go to each group—discussion directors, literary luminaries, and vocabulary enrichers—to explain further what I wanted them to do. (I should add here that my AP class is small, sixteen students at the time, so that even the role-alike groups were not very large. With a larger class, I might have two groups of discussion directors, two of literary luminaries, etc., preparing for the role-different groups they would ultimately break into.) As students prepared their questions, etc., I monitored the groups, answering questions when they had them, asking questions when they seemed "stuck" so that they would still do the thinking about what they would want to bring from the text to their small-group discussion. Since the students had been keeping reading logs, they all had explored issues of the story, to some extent, through their logs, and this made the sharing in these role-alike groups more productive.

After fifteen or twenty minutes in these role-alike groups, I asked students to move into the heterogeneous circles I had assigned. I told them to begin the discussion with a question and to incorporate key passages and vocabulary into the discussion to support their views. I wanted them to use what they had worked on in their role-alike groups but not to feel limited to that if their discussions led to questions, passages, and vocabulary not generated during that first fifteen-minute period. I monitored these small-group discussions mostly by sitting in and listening, offering a question here or there that might encourage them to extend their thoughts but mostly remaining silent as students quite successfully explored issues that I would have chosen had I been responsible for leading discussion in the traditional "teacher-centered" way. How much more meaningful this seemed to be!

I had determined at the outset that we would do literature circles throughout the tales, giving every student at least one or two opportunities to "be" each role and meet in a variety of small groups. After every couple of tales, we would meet as a whole group, not to explore every question that students had raised, for that was unnecessary, but instead to explore issues that they still needed to discuss or new issues that had surfaced during the small groups. I also brought in a few topics/questions related to some of the literary criticism about Chaucer that I wanted to share. Also, by the second tale, I introduced the role of capable connector to encourage students to look at some links among the tales, both style- and content-oriented. As students worked in literature circles over a period of days, they were always encouraged to explore their questions and to support ideas from text.

During the literature circle process for "The Wife of Bath's Tale" my teaching was being formally observed by the Assistant Principal for Instruction. The class was designed to go through the whole process I had set up: role-alike groups, then small, role-distinct groups, and finally whole-class discussion. This was the third tale with which I had used literature circles, so the students were becoming quite adept at them. However, as the teacher,

I am not always able to know what is going on in every group at each moment, because I'm listening to one group or asking questions of another or explaining something that is unclear, etc. This special "observer" gave me an opportunity to see/hear these literature circles in a different way, since her task was simply to listen to and watch what was happening.

Among the comments she heard coming from the small groups were these: "I think she was a bad wife, not because she was strong, but because she was mean." "The Wife was dominant in her relationships. Do you think there is always a dominant person in any relationship?" During the whole-group discussion, this is some of what she heard: "We were discussing if the Wife of Bath was a liberated woman, a woman of the nineties." "No, I don't think she represents a whole gender and certainly not women of the nineties, but when you look at the time she lived, women were treated really badly and maybe that's why she lived that way." "In the tale, no one argued with the knight so he must have represented the thinking of the time." The observer also commented that one boy, Jeff, "raised a question about the economics of the Wife's situation, suggesting that they might have as much to do with her behavior as personality." Other questions concerning whether the Wife was a feminist or an antifeminist, etc., were presented and would be explored the next day.

The observer was particularly impressed with the energy and enthusiasm "with which students attacked their discussions and in the quality of the interchanges." Furthermore, she saw that student ideas were at center stage and that their discussions were confident and directly aimed toward one another "without feeling the need to 'clear' responses with Mrs. Ward." She concluded that observing this class "was an energizing experience." I share these comments because while they are some testimony to my preparation with the students, they are mostly, I believe, proof of the effectiveness of literature circles. As someone who does much observation myself, I am often amazed at how much teacher-centered discussion still takes place in most English classrooms, regardless of ability level. I have been thrilled at the ownership the students have taken for their own learning since I began the use of literature circles. One student recently mentioned her work in literature circles in a personal essay she was writing in hopes of earning a scholarship. She said something about serving as a discussion director in her English class. . . .

I have not mentioned evaluation/assessment yet, other than the points for reading logs. I "assess" literature circles in a variety of ways, some direct, some indirect. First, I often collect the students' role sheets and award points for the thoroughness of their work, ten points or so. In addition, I monitor discussion participation by giving a +, ✓, or − on notecards; this is not time-consuming. Furthermore, I give tests and writing assignments that indirectly assess the value of the work done in literature circles.

Chapter I Study Skills

Let me begin by saying that using literature circles with "at risk" students is quite different from using them with AP students! While I realize this is not a revelation to anyone, it does require, I believe, a different approach to introducing literature circles and more perseverance from the teacher to "ensure" their success.

I teach one section of study skills, a Chapter I–funded program in which we are able to limit the number of students in each section to twelve. Still, these students can sometimes pack a punch like a class of twenty-five! Nevertheless, working with twelve bodies, particularly when running literature circles, is more manageable than working with larger numbers, so I believed I could have successful literature circles in this class, too. It's important to note, however, that students take study skills in place of a study hall and in addition to all their other classes, including English. Consequently, since the course is designed to address issues like note taking, study strategies, etc., in addition to allowing them some homework time, the time I can devote to something like literature circles or other types of presentation and discussion of literature is somewhat limited for each class period. In fact, I never take the entire period to present or work on a literature lesson. As a result, the preparation for a literature circle discussion and the actual discussion rarely take place in the same period.

I did not introduce the roles or the role sheets in my first attempt to prepare my study skills students for literature circles. Instead, I asked them each to write three things on a notecard in response to a short story ("The Dinner Party," by Mona Gardner) they had just read. I asked them to jot down a good discussion question, which I defined as a question about the story that could not be answered by yes or no. I also asked them to choose and write down a line or two of the story that they found interesting, funny, informative, descriptive, etc. Finally I asked them to choose one vocabulary word that was perhaps unfamiliar to them or that was repeated several times in the story, indicating it might be a key word. Students had little trouble with this and willingly did the work. Once I collected the cards, we had a brief, all-class discussion of the story using some of their questions, lines, and words and a few of my own questions as well.

The next day, based on the success of the previous day, I introduced another short story, "The Parsley Garden," by William Saroyan, a story about a boy who believes he was humiliated unnecessarily. Before asking the students to read the story, I asked them if they knew what "humiliated" meant and if they had ever been humiliated. This generated some good prereading discussion to whet their appetites to read about a boy who had been humiliated and had resolved the issue by the end of the story. I then began to read the story aloud, students following along, and I paused from time to time to ask a question or ask a student to make a prediction. After reading a couple of pages and arriving at a good I-wonder-what-happens-next point, I asked them to finish the rest of the story silently. Because of the obligation to provide time for them to work on their homework, I collected the stories when they were finished and told students we would get back to them the next day.

Discussions the next day were a little slow-going at first, and certainly not lengthy, but I basically wanted them to experience some exchange, some talk about the questions they had composed. I wasn't expecting AP-type discussion (yet), and I didn't get it. What I did see and hear, however, were some thoughtful and rather reflective comments in response to the following questions, which had been generated by students the day before: Why did Al steal the hammer? Why does he seem to hate the two guys so much? Why did he eat the parsley? (If you know the story, you'll probably be as impressed as I was that the kids asked this question, because Al's eating the parsley is deeply symbolic.) Why didn't he take the money from his mom? Why doesn't he feel humiliated anymore?

Had I taught this story in the traditional way where I generated the questions, I would have asked several or all of these questions. The students had done what I considered to be impressive work for the first time through, and I knew I would be able to do more with literature circles. Since that first time, I have done several other short stories with my study skills students using literature circles. Each time I have made some variations in how students prepare for them. Each time, too, I am more convinced that using literature circles can be effective with all students regardless of their ability level and can give students ownership of their learning in a way that traditional activities cannot.

Dickensian Circles in Ninth Grade

DONNA-MARIE STUPPLE, MAINE EAST HIGH SCHOOL, NILES IL

I began experimenting with literature circles for *Great Expectations* about two years ago, and I will try to give you a succinct overview (never my strong suit) so you can decide whether any of what I tried might fit your current teaching.

The roles were typical—word wizard, essence extractor, lit critic, etc. However, what may be different is that my kids worked in two kinds of groups sort of simultaneously. I established what I called *base groups* that remained consistent throughout the unit. My motive for these groups was to divide and conquer the difficult reading by having kids share summaries of particular chapters. One "reading chunk," for example, consisted of Chapters 14 to 19. Each person in the base group (usually five students) had to prepare a summary of only one chapter from the assigned chunk. On the day the reading was due, the base group met and each kid summarized his or her chapter in sequence. Summaries were to be spoken conversationally, not dictated slowly while everyone wrote down every word. The other kids made notes on overview sheets, and asked questions to clarify facts and relationships. By attending their base group meeting, kids "jigsawed" all five chapters to get the big picture of that day's reading. Each kid had actually read just one chapter and then heard summaries of the other four. Essentially, we were jigsawing the reading of this very challenging book.

The students received their assignment on a *chapter group* role assignment sheet. The project coordinator (discussion leader and organizer) dealt the sheets out to the base group members. No one could repeat a role. This was the more customary literature circle part of the procedure.

Once the summaries were completed in the base groups (one class period or so), then the chapter groups met for about two periods. Each chapter group had a word wizard, an illustrator, etc.—but all focused only on a single chapter. Because the sheets had been distributed randomly, the chapter groups had different members each time. Kids had a chance to mix around the class a lot, which I liked, while the base groups provided some consistency. At the end of their discussion, the project coordinator made sure the review sheet for the chapter was completed. The chapter illustration and the review sheet were posted on the bulletin board. In effect, we created an environmental *Cliffs Notes* around the classroom. Because I had two classes of accelerated freshmen working on this, we had two sets of sheets, another plus.

The small-group days were followed by whole-class discussion. I tried to base the periodic quizzes on topics from these discussions, but students sometimes blamed their inability to answer or to answer well on the bad summaries from so-and-so. Some of these complaints were typical grade griping, but some were legitimate.

The logistics probably seem complicated, and, to be truthful, as I look back, I dazzle myself by the Atwellian dimensions of the unit. A major sanity device was color coding: all the illustrators were pink, word wizards yellow, etc. To prepare a set of assignments, I grabbed a sheet of pink roles, filled in one chapter on each, and sliced them up for one base group. That automatically gave each kid in the base group a reading/summary assignment as well as a chapter group (literature circle) assignment. Sometimes a student received one long chapter, other times maybe two or three short ones. No time was wasted jockeying for roles in the base groups because they were always the same; it was also easier for me to make sure no group duplicated roles.

Good news, bad news? The bulletin board and subsequent "notebooking" of all the illustrations and summaries was a powerful statement about collaboration. I thought the unit involved more students more actively than any approach I had tried previously. Also, we moved through the novel with less (and different!) moaning and groaning.

I had used Chapters 1 and 8 as the model chapters, but I don't think I spent enough time practicing effective summary—how explicit to be, how to be explicit and still be concise—which is tricky to master in a rush. (In stage 2, I summarized some of the less important chapters to keep them out of the assignment pool.)

A minor plus: the kids' word wizard lists picked up almost all the words I had on my own lists from previous years. I used all the words turned in—I defined the one-shot words for them (not too much carryover value for reading) and assigned the others for our traditional vocabulary work.

Great Expectations is no longer part of the freshman curriculum (nothing to do with this experiment), so I didn't have another year to try out an improved version of the concept. I am trying text sets related to *Lord of the Flies,* however; the organizational challenges of groups don't deter me for long. Just this weekend, I started thinking of how I could apply literature circles to *Romeo and Juliet.* Think of the great roles—casting director, stage manager, etc. I suspect I will have only a single layer of groups this time around; middle age makes us prudent.

Artifact 1 (Figure 7–1): Schedule and Overview

Modeling and how-tos occurred in the first block of chapters. As I mentioned above, I underestimated the difficulty of summarizing Dickens—not just the style problem (which was one of my motivations for trying this approach in the first place), but the sorting and condensing that a skilled reader does almost effortlessly. Because the kids had live audiences, they were "questioned" into improving their summaries, but I think I could have eliminated some of the frustration by spending more time modeling the actual process of annotating. Also, we could have created a list of strategies for condensing their own writing.

Artifact 2 (Figure 7–2): Role Definitions

Pretty standard lit circle stuff. Note my new angle on vocabulary in the Word Wizard II assignment. Instead of collecting the esoteric words, we gathered examples of concrete verbs. In the course of the whole novel, every kid had an experience with each role.

Artifact 3 (Figure 7–3): Chapter Summary Sheet

I liked the column I added that encouraged students to identify the chapter's major purpose (a who? chapter focused on characters, a where? chapter clarified setting, etc.). It didn't always work, of course, but it nudged the freshmen toward a more analytic frame of mind.

Artifact 4 (Figure 7–4): Chapter Group Report

This little sheet just gave the project coordinator a checklist for the task of making sure everyone was on target. I liked it as a way to see that everyone was pulling his or her own weight. The group context and the bulletin boards were prime motivators; no one asked about grades for the posted work (miraculous in itself—these were honors freshmen!).

Figure 7–1   Schedule and Overview

Stage 1

Introduction to Great Expectations *Literature Circles and Modeling of Group Tasks*

Chapters 1–6, 8
Everyone reads Chapters 1 through 6 and Chapter 8.
Base group:
• Reviews individual summaries.
• Submits unanswered questions, discussion topics for full-class attention.

Chapters 7–13
Base group distributes chapter assignments, one to each member. *Write your name on your assignment file sheet when you complete it.*
Homework:
• Each member has to read *only* the assigned chapter.
• Each member prepares a summary that includes specific names and events as well as a clear idea of the beginning and end of the chapter.
• Each member also completes the specific role task for the assigned chapter.

Stage 2

Chapters 14–19
Same procedure as above *but* make sure you get a different task for your chapter (different color).

Class Time Plan

Day 1   Base groups meet to share summaries and fill in summary sheets.
Days 2/3 Chapter groups work on specific tasks together.
Day 4   Full-class discussion of issues raised.
Day 5   Review quiz/vocabulary.

Figure 7–2   Role Definitions

Project Coordinator: Chapter_____   Name_____

You're responsible for keeping everyone on task, leading the discussion while the group decides on procedures for getting the tasks done, checking on progress, and troubleshooting. Not enough? Okay, you also make sure that the reports are posted and filed.

Quotable Quoter: Chapter_____   Name_____

Select a sentence or passage that captures the chapter and/or that pleases you for its phrasing, idea, etc. Work with the Lit Critic to complete the Chapter Review Sheet that will be posted under the illustration for this chapter.

Lit Critic: Chapter_____   Name_____

How does this chapter fit into the novel as a whole? Why is it significant? What does it provide in terms of character motivation or development, plot or subplot, setting, theme or major ideas? Even if you were going to condense (or eliminate!) this chapter, what would you definitely have to keep in the novel somewhere? What does the chapter add to your ideas about (appreciation of?) "the Dickensian style"?

Essence Illustrator: Chapter_____   Name_____

You make up a title for the chapter and include it in your illustration (collage, line drawing, cartoon, computer graphic, etc.) that will be posted on the bulletin board in the back.

Word Wizard I: Chapter_____   Name_____

Find six to eight unfamiliar or unclear words in your chapter. Test the words out on your chapter group to select the best two or three for the class list.

Word Wizard II: Chapter_____   Name_____

New angle on vocabulary: find eight to ten good verbs.*
Write down the verb and enough of the context to let us see how it's used. (Chapter group will select their four favorites.)

*What's a good verb?
    An action word (not "is," "was," etc.)
    A precise description ("slouch" over "sit")
    Understood by most readers (dictionary not needed)

Figure 7–3   Chapter Summary Sheet

Chapter / Who? What? Where? Why? / Annotation / Vocabulary

_____

_____

_____

_____

_____

_____

_____

_____

Figure 7–4   Chapter Group Report

Chapter(s) _____

Project Coordinator: _____

☐ Chapter Illustration/Title Posted

Essence Extractor: _____

☐ Chapter Overview Posted

Lit Critic: _____

Quotes: _____

_____

_____

_____

_____

_____

☐ Vocabulary Words Listed at Bottom of Sheet

Word Wizard: _____

Vocabulary Words: _____

_____

_____

_____

_____

_____

_____

Figure 7–5   Chapter Review Sheet

Lines worth rereading:

_____

_____

. . . and why:

_____

_____

About the chapter:

_____

_____

Issues and Ideas:

_____

_____

Prepared by:

_____

_____

Reading Circles in a College Criminology Class

MARLINE PEARSON, MADISON AREA TECHNICAL COLLEGE, MADISON, WI

I teach at a two-year technical college and have been using literature circles—which I renamed reading circles—for three semesters with my criminology classes. I have two sections of forty-five to fifty students each. Frankly, I've never witnessed such engaged, enthusiastic, and serious discussion among so many students in a classroom in my fifteen years of teaching. This testimony comes not only from what I have observed by walking around and listening to my students as they talk in their reading circles, but also from reading the process checker sheets that each student fills out about their experience with the circles.

Let me add that my skill with reading circles has evolved over time. Three semesters ago, I was pretty positive about reading circles, but my students' experience with this technique has improved each semester as I've begun to troubleshoot and work out the bugs. There are several things I've learned from my mistakes and oversights in using this strategy over the past three semesters, and I'd like to share them.

Tell Your Students Why You Value Reading Circles

At the outset, I spend some time explaining why we're doing reading circles and why I value them. In fact, this leads me into a short discourse on my philosophy of learning and teaching, which values student-generated as opposed to teacher-directed discussion. Reading circles start with what the students think about the reading. They give students the chance to answer the following sorts of questions: Which passages are meaningful, puzzling, controversial, or striking and why? What connections occur in your mind as you read—to your own life or what you've read or heard about? What feeling does it evoke in you and how do you express it visually? Finally, what big issues and questions does the reading raise? My experience is that students really like this format because they feel they truly are discussing what's on their mind.

I also try to acknowledge that students have rarely had the opportunity to do this in class and that some may have had lousy experiences with class discussion. Typically, teachers set the discussion questions and issues and often don't give much time for students to think about their responses. This encourages passivity and a just-look-up-the-answers approach. It fosters the opposite of authentic or critical thinking. I'm always amazed how so many students can go through school and never really get any encouragement for authentic thoughts.

I always tell my students: "To do my job as a teacher and facilitate learning, I need to know about your thoughts, your experiences, the connections you make, and the meaning that you give to class materials. Above all, I need to know the questions that are important to you. Learning is a process of connecting new information to current knowledge and experience you possess." Unfortunately, too much teaching is like "bulldozing"— that is, the teacher plows through the material without stopping to check out how students are experiencing it. In the end, far too many students are silenced rather than stimulated by their experience in the classroom. Reading circles are a good tool, I think, for fostering some genuine discussion and giving me a sense of how learners experience ideas.

I also tell my students that I personally value collaborative work and that we all need practice in this. We need practice listening to one another to develop our own thinking. I explain that I will be circulating around and that they should flag me immediately if they need any clarification on roles. I point out that because each role reflects a different learning style, some roles may feel natural and others awkward. The bottom line, I tell them, is that I want the circles to work and to feel useful to them. If they don't work, then we need to try something else.

Starting Right: Train Your Students Well

Probably the most important thing I've learned over the past couple of years is the necessity of thoroughly training students in the reading circle process and then demonstrating it. My first experience using reading circles was literally the day after I myself was introduced to it. I rushed out and tried it with my students, doing minimal training and virtually no role modeling. Of the eight groups, five worked very well, despite the lack of training. But still, having three groups of disgruntled and/or confused students is not a pleasant situation. I have now worked out a fairly efficient way to train students and model the process with the class. It takes one or two class periods, but it is well worth the effort. And the training can be done on the material you want them to read anyway. This semester, after paying close attention to training, I can report that every single group was highly functional and engaged from the start. As of this writing, the groups are on their third round of reading circles and their enthusiasm and success are still holding.

How I Train Students

I give students a two-page article to take home and read. The next day in class I announce I'm going to train them to do reading circles and explain what they are and why I value them. I pass out the master sheets describing the roles and go over them with the class. Then I divide the class in half. Half the class is told that they will have ten minutes to go over the article (which they've already read the night before), pick out two passages that they find meaningful, and then jot down their reasons for picking them.

Meanwhile, the other half of the class is told to go over the article and jot down one or two creative connections. I choose these two roles because they are often the most confusing. After ten minutes, I ask for volunteers to share their chosen passages and elaborate on them. I then invite others to respond to the passage masters. We might review four or five passages before going on to review creative connections in the same way. I find that one student's passage or connection tends to evoke a response or idea from another student. Before we know it, we're into a good discussion on the article and the whole class now knows what was meant by those two roles.

My role in all of this is that of discussion director and facilitator: I invite everyone's participation, bring the groups back to the topic if they wander off too long, and stay aware of the time limits we've set for the group. I also point out that the discussion director's job is to come to the group with one, two, or three big issues or questions that the article raises. Using the overhead projector, I write/show them four issues that I would raise as the discussion director for this particular article. I advise them that the discussion director should *not* immediately start the group with her or his prepared topics, since these issues may come out naturally in the course of the students' discussion of passages and connections. In the beginning, I discovered that discussion directors tended to take on too much of the responsibility for selecting issues. I suggest they simply stand ready to raise their questions if they don't naturally arise in the course of the discussion.

During this initial training, the other role I assume is that of illustrator. I display a transparency drawing that I have done for the article and then ask the students to interpret it. Because I'm not very artistic, they quickly get the point that we're talking about expression, not about great "art" when it comes to the illustrator role. This approach helps my students relax about being the illustrator—an important consideration, since almost all of them initially blanch at having to draw. After my funny introduction to this role and their practice with it, I discovered that the role had become very popular. By the second round of reading circles, my students were asking me to tape their illustrations to the wall. My classroom became decorated in a unique and delightful fashion, and all of the students had a good time looking at all the drawings.

This "fun" approach to reading circles also helps the students understand that the goal is to have a natural, free-flowing discussion of what *they* understand from the readings. I tell them not to be totally driven by the roles, they are just there to help. I also keep reminding them that they are to be active listeners and that they need to respond to the things others say. This is something we also track with the process checker sheets.

At the end of the training, I give the students a two-page article, put them in groups, and let them divide up the roles. They are asked to prepare roles for reading circles for the next class period. I tell them I'll be checking at the door for their role preparation.

One final note about training: expect that it will take a while to smooth out the rough edges of your own experience with reading circles. It is new for you, the teacher, as well as for the students. Stay with it and you will be rewarded.

Metacognitive Tracking with the Process Checker Sheet

I've found it very useful to allow the students some time to reflect, do some self-evaluation, and then write something short about the discussion in their reading circle. Over three semesters, I've undergone a change of thinking on the process checker sheets. When I was first introduced to the original literature circles model, the process checker evaluation sheet was filled out by only one group member, who then evaluated each member of the group. I modified it so that each group member filled out a sheet with qualitative comments on the discussion as well as an evaluation of herself or himself and the other members of the circle. I have now given up the evaluation of other members. I guess in the beginning I thought I had to do this—almost as if it were a way of saying, "Participate or else!" My thinking now is that if students don't really get into it, then why do it? It's useful to me as long as it's useful to students. Also, I feel that if there was a problem earlier, it was probably more my fault for not training the students, clarifying the process, or allowing the students enough time and practice to do well.

Now into my third semester, I am into my third version of process checker sheets—a version that requires my students to evaluate only their own participation. This sheet basically asks the student to respond yes or no to the question of whether or not the discussion worked—that is, was there some genuine "connection" with one another's thoughts and ideas? If the answer is no, then students are asked to try to write about why they think this connecting did not happen. I offer some possible reasons: lack of preparation, boring article, different personalities or learning styles, etc. I hope that these suggestions will give students more freedom to be honest. If the answer is yes, then they are asked to describe one or two of the high points of the discussion, the topics or questions the group really latched on to. At the bottom of the checker sheet, they are to evaluate their own participation with a plus, an equal sign (meaning so-so), or a minus.

After the students have completed their self-evaluations, I collect the sheets by group and clip them together. I review them immediately to see if the group is working well. What I read on the checker sheets tells me what the "hot" issues are and thus tells me what to focus on in the rest of my teaching. For example, I might use some of the students' comments in a reading circle to start off the next class. This clear attention to what the students think is important—as well as the notes I write on each checker sheet when I return it to the student—indicates to the student how seriously I value the effort expended in a reading circle. It is probably especially important that a teacher take the time to write comments back to the students. My own comments are nonjudgmental and nonevaluative. I just share a reaction or ask clarifying questions. I tell the students that these sheets are the clearest way for me to gauge the usefulness of this format and to tap into what they're talking about.

In short, I really like my latest checker sheets because they offer the student some time for reflection and clarification of ideas as well as for a bit of metacognitive work. They give students the chance to write about the content and the process of their own discussions.

Other Important Tips

It is important to start small by using short, one- or two-page articles. Moreover, although reading circles do not need to be done every class period or even every week, students do need to practice the techniques thoroughly if they are to gain the skill it takes to make reading circles worthwhile. Do reading circles shortly after training the students and then do them again within a week or two.

Don't underestimate—as I did in the beginning—how much time students need to flourish in a session of reading circles. When I first tried them, I tended to frustrate students by ending the group meetings too soon. Either give students more time—it shows you are really serious about authentic student discussion—or give them shorter pieces to discuss. Preparing roles at home also saves time.

It certainly helps to check role preparations at the door and then give the students real consequences for not being prepared, including not getting credit, sitting outside the groups, or not being permitted in the classroom until they have completed their role preparation. After I did this a few times in my classroom, everyone got the message and I didn't need to do it anymore. It's important to remember what we as teachers are up against when we institute reading circles. In trying to create a more active classroom, we are attempting nothing less than a change in educational culture. Thus we should hardly be surprised if a number of students are resistant to reading circles in the beginning. Aside from its being a new and frightening thing to do, many students have had bad experiences with classroom discussions and collaborative activities. Although well-planned and well-executed collaboration can be wonderful for everyone involved, we all know how frustrating a sloppily planned and carried-out collaborative activity can be. Good collaboration takes the careful planning and monitoring of a skillful teacher.

Finally, a tip about student absences: a source of hesitation on the part of many teachers in using collaboration is their concern for the effects of absences on group cohesion. One way to deal with absences is to give credit (points) for participation in reading circles. Students can still get credit if they phone a circle member and ask that person to carry their role to the group. The person they call must be willing to jot down the role preparation of the absentee and discuss it over the phone in order to be able to relay it to the group effectively. So far, this has worked very well for me. To be sure, I can imagine situations where someone might abuse the privilege, but I think the other students would put a stop to this on their own; if not, I would intervene.

CHAPTER EIGHT

• • • • • • • • •

Record Keeping, Evaluation, and Grading

WHEN GROUPS of students are spending large chunks of the day meeting in literature circles, teachers often worry, How can I evaluate this activity? How do I know what kids are learning? What records do I need to keep? How can I give grades? And what about report cards? These same concerns, of course, arise in connection with almost *any* cooperative, inquiry-based activity in which student groups work without direct supervision while the teacher facilitates. At one level, these questions reflect a genuine concern about how teachers can document kids' growth, as well as eventually award a justifiable grade.

At another level, questions like these probably also reflect concern about classroom management and discipline. After all, grades are very often used as a mechanism of control in the classroom, with the reward of a high grade or the threat of a low one being used to shape children's behavior in school. When teachers think about decentralizing their classrooms in the ways that literature circles require—with kids working largely on their own—they start wanting a list of contingencies to employ if individuals or groups aren't productive. That's why, in Chapter 4, we talked at length about problems of classroom management in literature circles. Teachers interested in keeping their assessment system separate from their discipline system might want to have a look at that section.

Assessment of Literature Circles

Literature circles leave a very rich trail of evidence of kids' reading, learning, and thinking—if we know how to recognize, capture, and talk about all this data meaningfully. Luckily, our ability to gather and understand such information has recently taken a big leap ahead. In the past several years there has been an exciting and timely revolution in the field of educational evaluation. Important books on the authentic assessment of literacy activities have been published by people like Rob Tierney, Ken and Yetta Goodman, Susan Glazer, Lynn Rhodes, and others. This burgeoning body of research and practical classroom models helps us all to develop more accurate, sophisticated, and meaningful pictures of what kids know and are able to do. While we'll now go on to share several assessment strategies developed specifically for literature circles by our own network, teachers who want more details and models should consult the bibliography at the end of this chapter.

To begin with, we must approach the assessment of literature circles as we would any other complex, integrated classroom activity. Anything we do in the name of assessment must be theoretically congruent with the collaborative, student-centered nature of the instructional model. So we have to start with the questions, What are we assessing for? When we observe, record, measure, or judge, what are we trying to accomplish? What theories and principles guide our assessment efforts? To frame these issues, we have listed below some guiding principles of sound, authentic assessment. Later, we offer some specific ways to assess students in literature circles according to these standards.

1. Assessment should reflect and encourage *good instruction*. At the very least, the evaluation of student work should never distort or harm solid classroom practice. Ideally, assessment activities should unequivocally reinforce progressive curriculum and learner-centered teaching methods.

2. The best assessment activities are actually *integral parts of instruction*. While many traditional measures occur separate from or after teaching, the most powerful new assessment activities—such as conferences, analytic scoring scales, and portfolios—*are* ingredients of good instruction. When assessment overlaps with instruction in this way, it helps teachers to be more effective in same amount of instructional time.

3. Powerful evaluation efforts focus on the major, whole, *outcomes* valued in the curriculum: real, complex performances of writing, researching, reading, experimenting, problem solving, creating, speaking, etc. Traditional assessment has been largely devoted to checking whether students are receiving the proper "inputs," the alleged building blocks, basics, or

subskills. The new assessment paradigm dares to focus on the big payoffs, the highest-order outcomes of education, in which kids orchestrate big chunks of learning in realistic applications.

4. Most school assessment activities should be *formative.* This means that we assess primarily to ensure that students learn better and teachers teach more effectively. *Summative evaluation,* which involves translating students' growth to some kind of grade that can be reported outside the classroom, is just one small, narrow, and occasional element of a comprehensive, contemporary assessment program.

5. Skillful and experienced evaluators take a *developmental perspective.* They are familiar with the major growth models, both general cognitive stage theories and the models from specific curriculum fields (stages of reading, mathematical thinking, invented spelling, etc). Rather than checking students against arbitrary age or grade level targets, teachers track the story of each child's individual growth through developmental phases.

6. Traditional norm-referenced, competitive measures that rank students against one another (such as letter grades and numerically scored tests) provide little helpful formative assessment and tend to undermine progressive instruction. Instead, constructive programs increasingly rely on *self-referenced growth measures,* where each student is compared with herself or himself. This means teachers must have ways of valuing, tracking, and recording such individualized factors as improvement, effort, good faith, insight, risk taking, rate of change, and energy.

7. Teachers need a rich *repertoire of assessment strategies* to draw from in designing sensitive, appropriate evaluation activities for particular curriculum areas. Among these broad strategies are:

Kidwatching/Anecdotal Records: open-ended, narrative observational notes, logs, and records.
Checklists: structured, curriculum-anchored observation guides, charts, and records.
Interviews/Conferences: face-to-face conversation to access, track, and monitor student growth.
Portfolios/Work Samples: writing, art, projects, video/audiotapes, learning logs, student journals, etc.

Performance Assessment: criteria and instruments used for analytic scoring of complex performances.

Classroom Tests: teacher-made achievement measures, tests, worksheets, etc.

8. It is never enough to look at learning events from only one angle; rather, we now use *multiple measures,* examining students' learning growth from several different perspectives as outlined above. By *triangulating* assessments, we get a "thick" picture of kids' learning, ensuring that unexpected growth, problems, and side effects are not missed.

9. A key trait of effective thinkers, writers, problem solvers, readers, researchers, and other learners is that they constantly self-monitor and self-evaluate. Therefore, a solid assessment program must consistently help (and require) students to take increasing responsibility for their own record keeping, metacognitive reflection, and *self-assessment.*

10. It takes *many different people working cooperatively* to evaluate student growth and learning effectively. In every classroom, there should be a balance between external assessment (district standardized tests, state assessments, etc.), teacher-run evaluation, student self-evaluation, parent involvement in assessment, and collaborative assessments involving various of these parties.

11. Teachers need to *reallocate the considerable time they already spend on assessment*—evaluation, record keeping, testing, and grading activities. They need to spend less time scoring and more time saving and documenting student work. Instead of creating and justifying long strings of numbers in their grade books, teachers can collect and save samples of kids' original, unscored products. This reallocation of time means that once they are installed, new assessment procedures don't require any more time of teachers than the old ways—nor any less.

12. Sound evaluation programs provide, where necessary, a data base for deriving *legitimate, defensible student grades.* However, major national curriculum groups have recommended that competitive, norm-referenced grading should be deemphasized and replaced by the many richer kinds of assessments outlined above (see Zemelman, Daniels, and Hyde 1993).

13. The currently available state and national standardized tests yield an exceedingly narrow and unreliable picture of student achievement, are poor indicators of school performance, and encourage archaic instructional

practices. Therefore, professional teachers *avoid "teaching to standardized tests."* Instead, they show colleagues, parents, and administrators the more sophisticated, detailed, accurate, and meaningful assessments they have developed for their own classrooms.

Assessing Kids' Growth in Literature Circles

All of the above principles suggest that literature circles naturally *invite* the use of state-of-the-art assessment approaches. Indeed, most of the teachers whose classrooms we've visited in this book have developed assessment tools and strategies that embody these progressive ideals. These teachers take seriously the precept of triangulation, and so they use a *variety* of assessment tools to create a deep picture of the whole activity (which is talking about books). Further, since lit circles are mainly a student-led, independent activity, these teachers encourage lots of student self-assessment. Here are some of the most common and effective approaches to assessment in literature circles.

Observation

When the teacher pays his occasional visits to each literature circle, he has a natural opportunity to assess the progress of both individuals and the group. Some teachers like to use a simple *checklist* for this purpose, keyed either to the role sheets being used or to the names of students in the group. Such a checklist might include yes/no items such as "Brought book and role sheet to the group," "Played role effectively," "Contributed to the group's productivity," "Listened attentively," "Built upon the contributions of others," and the like. Other teachers have developed a rubric of formal performance criteria and use a *scaled scoring sheet* to rate the whole group's effectiveness on one or more official visits. Other teachers prefer to take *open-ended observational notes,* jotting down important or memorable comments made by kids, as well as noting reactions to the process of the group.

Still other teachers find it obtrusive and threatening to invade a group and then sit silently, rating students. Instead, these teachers stop *between* groups to make their notes privately, before the impressions slip away. Teachers making this last choice may get to fewer groups each day, but will be able to more fully join in the groups they do visit. Perhaps when teachers visit a literature circle group, they should come first and foremost as fellow readers, fully open to being captivated by the book under discussion, the kids in the group, and the ideas at hand. To be visibly torn between the role of evaluator and the role of fellow reader may undermine a teacher's fellowship with students in ways we cannot readily see. And, unless grading is a constant and official demand in a particular school, there's no *reason* to visit groups in the evaluator role when being a coach, model, and partner is so much more powerful.

Conferences

Some teachers have periodic *individual reading conferences* with students, and one good topic for these conferences is the child's literature circle. Teachers can talk with the students about their own role in the group, the circle's problems and pleasures, and about the group's handling of specific books and ideas. Such a conversation helps the teacher access children's thinking directly and personally, and the information gained can help with everything from future book choices to re-forming the groups. Most teachers keep simple notes on these conferences, so they can reflect on them later in reconstructing patterns of growth, talking to parents, or arriving at grades.

Teachers can also conduct *group conferences with the literature circles* themselves. The teacher visits each group as the group is finishing up a book, asking the group to set aside one meeting in which they will reflect back together over what they have accomplished. At these meetings, kids review both the content of the book, the interpretations they have given it, and the process of their work as a group. As with an individual conference, teachers might let this meeting unfold spontaneously or work from a set list of questions they want to hear addressed. Similarly, they may want to make some notes during or after the conference—or simply tape-record the group conference and put a copy of the tape in each child's portfolio. This last alternative relieves the teacher of record keeping during the meeting, and as long as the goal of the conference has been to document and not to grade the group's work, simply *saving* the resulting tape may be plenty of "assessment." Once kids have learned the purposes and procedures of such assessments, they can tape and critique group meetings for *themselves*. Groups can review the tape, make notes, and then have a special session to evaluate their own process. Finally, each kid can put a copy of his or her own written report in a personal portfolio. All these variations are good examples of how good assessment can actually be part of rather than separate from valuable class activities.

Artifacts

The role sheets that help set students' purposes for reading and that guide the group meetings are also artifacts teachers can collect and (occasionally) study to note the sophistication of kids' thinking, the completeness of their preparation, or any other factor revealed by the sheets. There is no need to devise a separate test or worksheet when this item is a natural, daily by-product and record of the group's work. The same is true of the literature logs created by students in literature circle classrooms where sheets have been discarded in favor of open-ended journals. Here, the teacher may elect to collect kids' logs on a regular basis to track their reading and study their thinking. Some teachers also conduct separate teacher-student dialogue journals, so that kids are talking about their reading both orally with their group and in writing with their teacher. Obviously, such dialogue journals provide a rich source of insight for the teacher.

Portfolios

Some lit circle teachers use a folder or portfolio system, in which kids save everything related to their reading of a book: their unedited daily role sheets, their log entries, and whatever project or extension activity culminated the reading (this might be a videotape of a readers theater performance, a written report, an artwork, or other project). This portfolio of evidence provides a deep description of what the child has read and said and thought. While the individual pieces in this portfolio are not scored or graded, the portfolio collects raw material—evidence and documentation of the student's reading, thinking, and participation.

Projects

Many literature circle teachers assign groups some kind of culminating project following each book read, both to celebrate and synthesize the reading and to "promote" books so others in the class may select them in the future. While projects can be done in teams—and are often more energizing when done that way—this is also a time when individual work can be spun off (even to the point of yielding an individual grade, if the school situation requires it). Thus, after working in the literature circles for a couple of weeks, each student might go off to write their own Siskel-and-Ebert-style review, giving lots of reasons for their "thumbs up" or "thumbs down" rating. This piece of individual work can then be evaluated according to the teacher's or school's customary criteria.

A Note on Record Keeping

Many teachers who are just beginning to use innovations like literature circles sometimes worry excessively about evaluation and grades. Perhaps because they are stepping out of the instructional mainstream, they feel obligated to keep meticulous written records of everything that kids do, say, write, read, or think. They feel ashamed if their records are jumbled and fragmentary, they feel inferior to colleagues whose records are more orderly, and they may even experience paranoid delusions of angry parents demanding to see "justification" for a child's disputed grade in this weird new "experimental" activity.

So, as you implement literature circles and find yourself worrying about record keeping, remember: doing the activity is the main thing. Very adequate documentation of kids' growth in this activity—or any other classroom structure—can be achieved by occasionally sampling their performance, by collecting the raw material of their efforts in portfolios, by talking to kids regularly and keeping track of what they say. While long lines of marks in a grade book may seem more scientific, you can also trust your memory, your impressions of kids. Your thoughts and judgments are not unanchored—you have valid, important, and consistent criteria inside you.

And while we're on the subject, who says that *teachers* should be doing most or all of the record keeping? Piling all the paperwork on teachers is one of those unexamined elements of schooling that, ironically, breeds dependency and helplessness among students. If there are records worth keeping in literature circles, they are worth being kept by kids. Students can keep track of their own role sheets, keep their own folders updated, enter metacognitive reflections in their reading response logs, write self-assessments at the end of each book, bind and save their own projects, and so on.

If all else fails and you feel yourself coming down with the left-brain flu, here are a couple of prescriptions:

- If a record-keeping procedure interferes with your relationships with children, get rid of it.

- If a record-keeping procedure interferes with natural conversation in the literature circles, get rid of it.
- If a record-keeping procedure becomes an end in itself, get rid of it.
- If a record-keeping procedure is eating up so much of your time that you come to literature circles or (to school in general) stressed and upset, get rid of it.

Grading

In some schools and districts, the progressive, student-centered, collaborative activities of literature circles still must be fitted into a traditional assessment system that continues to mandate letter/number grades and/or class rankings. Is it possible to grade students for their work in literature circles? Yes—but as we have just seen, needing to assign a grade does not require the constant intrusion of scoring, points, or tests into the daily interaction of the circles. If kids are really "hooked on books" and working well with one another, we don't need any grades for management purposes, and we only need to sample their performance occasionally to feed the school system whatever grades it requires. Since we also want to sponsor a high level of self-evaluation and involve students in keeping their own records, whatever system we devise should have a strong, authentic component of student self-evaluation. Once again, as with all student-directed activities, it's best not to grade literature circle work at all. If at all possible, derive your formal grades from other activities, so that you don't undermine the genuineness of conversation in literature circles—and don't replace the collaborative culture you're trying to build with competition.

Some Grading Alternatives

How have some of the teachers visited in this book solved the problem of grading? Some use a daily "binary" grading system, and here's how it works. If a kid comes to a literature circle session with their sheet ready and their book in hand, and then joins in their group effectively, they get a check, a plus, or ten points. If not, they get a zero. In this grading system, there are no eights or nines (those are the distinctions that eat up teachers time in "justifying" and debating with grade-crazed students or parents). Once students know what they have to do to get the ten points, they

Figure 8–1 Literature Circles Evaluation Form

	Trait	Source of Data
40%	*Productivity*	
	Quantity of reading	Daily role sheets
	Preparation for discussions	Teacher observation
	Contributions to group	
40%	*Growth*	
	Variety of books, authors, genres	Daily role sheets
	Explanations and interpretations	Conferences
	Use of input from peers/teacher	Teacher observation
	Application of new skills and insights	Artifacts
	to next book	Projects
	Response expressed in projects	
20%	*Quality of Reading*	
	Difficulty of texts read	Teacher observation
	Level of thinking shown	Conferences
	Leadership in group sessions	Artifacts
	Sophistication of projects	Portfolios

generally do it—or accept the consequences when they flub. This daily performance grade can then be added up to a point total that counts as a given percentage of the overall grade. The rest of the grade is based upon whatever criteria the teacher and students identify as meaningful—often a project or a report—and is triangulated with the various other assessment techniques in use: kidwatching, checklists, formal performance assessment, group or individual conferences, etc.

Figure 8–1 is one performance assessment scale being used, with individual variations, by several Chicago-area teachers who are required by their districts to somehow assign students grades for their lit circles participation. In this scoring scale, the grade is derived from three ingredients: productivity, growth, and quality. The first two criteria, totaling 80 percent of the grade, are self-referenced measures—they compare the kid to self, not others. The other 20 percent—the "quality" assessment—*is* a norm-referenced measure, which basically says, "Compared to the rest of the kids in this class, the level of this child's reading/thinking is so-and-so."

Usually, both the student and the teacher would fill out a copy of this form, and then meet in conference to iron out any differences. The resulting point total for the lit circle component of the grading period can then be averaged in with other quantitative reading grades and eventually translated to the required report card categories. The teachers using this scale have made a small, but not complete, concession to their schools' hunger for some kind of comparative, kid-versus-kid grading. But they have also retained their own personal observation and judgment as the main source for grades.

Resources on Alternative Assessment

Anthony, Robert, Terry Johnson, Norma Mickelson, and Alison Preece. 1991. *Evaluating Literacy: A Perspective for Change.* Portsmouth, NH: Heinemann.

Balanoff, Pat, and Marcia Dickson. 1991. *Portfolios: Process and Product.* Portsmouth, NH: Boynton/Cook.

Daly, Elizabeth. 1990. *Monitoring Children's Language Development: Holistic Assessment in the Classroom.* Portsmouth, NH: Heinemann.

Glazer, Susan Mandel, and Carol Brown. 1993. *Portfolios and Beyond: Collaborative Assessment in Reading and Writing.* Norwood, MA: Christopher-Gordon.

Goodman, Kenneth, Yetta Goodman, and Wendy Hood. 1989. *The Whole Language Evaluation Book.* Portsmouth, NH: Heinemann.

Harp, Bill, ed. 1991. *Assessment and Evaluation in Whole Language Programs.* Norwood, MA: Christopher-Gordon.

Herman, Joel, Pamela Aschbacher, and Lynn Winters. 1992. *A Practical Guide to Alternative Assessment.* Alexandria, VA: Association for Supervision and Curriculum Development.

Rhodes, Lynn. 1993. *Literacy Assessment: A Handbook of Instruments.* Portsmouth, NH: Heinemann.

Rhodes, Lynn, and Nancy Shanklin. 1993. *Windows into Literacy: Assessing Learners K–8.* Portsmouth, NH: Heinemann.

Tierney, Robert, Mark Carter, and Laura Desai. 1991. *Portfolio Assessment in the Reading-Writing Classroom.* Norwood, MA: Christopher-Gordon.

CHAPTER NINE

• • • • • • • • •

Literature Circles in Context: What Happens the Rest of the Day?

W E ' V E   B E E N   T A L K I N G so far mostly about how to set up and run a fraction of the school day, week, and year—the part devoted to literature circles. But the question also arises, what *else* goes on during those days, weeks, and years? What other kinds of activities, structures, and strategies are complementary with literature circles?

To begin with, we must acknowledge that all teachers face some constraints—and some teachers face *lots* of them. Building your dream schedule is one thing, but real school life is usually tempered by curriculum mandates, standardized tests, pullout programs, school assemblies, departmental requirements, and the schedules of special teachers. Teachers do what they have to, and what they can.

But when we step back and idealize, trying to plan the perfect schedule, what ingredients go into the larger "whole language day?" First of all, it's good to remember, as we have been eloquently reminded by Carole Edelsky, Bess Altwerger, and Barbara Flores (1990), by Ken Goodman (1986), and by others, that holistic education is a *philosophy,* a closely interlocking set of ideas about teaching and learning. But it is also a philosophy in action. Progressive classrooms are characterized by certain distinctive *activities.* Whole language teachers tend to spend their time with students in certain recurrent patterns. Interestingly, many of these patterns, which I call *fundamental recurrent activities,* are structures that inherently scaffold interaction in the classroom.

- Reading aloud/storytelling
- Shared book experience
- Partner/buddy reading
- Independent reading/reading workshop/sustained silent reading

- Guided reading (structured, teacher-directed activities—demonstrations of reading process strategies)
- *Literature circles*
- Sharing and celebrating reading (readers theater, book-walks, book-talks, projects, reports, etc.)
- Language experience (for primary kids)
- Reading and writing across the curriculum (text sets, learning logs, clustering, brainstorming)
- Teacher-student conferences on reading and writing
- Teacher writing
- Independent writing/writing workshop/personal journals
- Dialogue journals/written conversations
- Guided ("process") writing (demonstrations of writing process strategies)
- Peer writing groups/kid conferences (peer editing, editors table)
- Sharing and publishing student writing (the author's chair/circle).

These are the activities one typically sees when visiting the classrooms of teachers who align themselves with "whole language" or "best practice." But this is just a collection of structures, mechanisms for deploying students, time, space, materials, and assistance.

The missing ingredient, the element that brings shape and depth and continuity to schooling, is *themes*. These are the broad, meaningful, important topics of inquiry that teachers and kids identify together and that provide the context for long-term, rich inquiry. Depending on the age and interests of the students and the expertise of the teacher, themes can be anything from insects to Scandinavia, from change to the future, from AIDS to the planets. I agree wholeheartedly with curriculum theorists Jim Beane (1991) and Alfie Kohn (1993) that these themes should be democratically identified and negotiated with students, not just announced by the teacher or mandated by the curriculum guide. Of course it's easier for teachers to keep repeating the themes that have worked before—after all, most of us have files of well-proven, kid-pleasing, preplanned units ready to go. But motivation, investment, and energy—not to mention the experience of democracy and decision making—are much deeper when the whole group sets up inquiries together. One side effect of the negotiated curriculum is that teachers are put back in the role of learner. When you let kids pick the themes, you probably won't be doing your teddy bears unit for the seventeenth year in a row.

So, together, themes and structures are the tools with which master teachers design days, weeks, years of learning for children. Taken together, a set of themes and the repertoire of key classroom activities is like an artist's palette; these are the colors that artful teachers paint with. Everyone doesn't use all the colors or the same colors or the same patterns—every combination is, and always should be, unique. The artistry of teaching is in the picture each teacher creates.

Two Kinds of Time: Guided and Independent

Of course, one of the attributes of great artworks, along with originality and creativity, is *balance*. In our schools, the most critical and neglected balance is the one between teacher-directed and student-sponsored learning. Teachers need to think about and plan for days that include both kinds of learning: guided and independent. While it is sometimes possible for the two to overlap in healthy ways, the history of American education is the history of the near-total dominance of one mode over the other. So, for the time being, for purposes of clarifying and redressing this overwhelming imbalance, it feels necessary to look at these two kinds of time as polar, black-and-white opposites.

Throughout this book we've asserted the need for regularly scheduled, sacred, protected, inviolate time for all kids, K–12, to do their own reading and writing and investigating—to read books, write pieces, and undertake inquiries they have chosen for themselves, alone and in groups. Such student-directed time may be facilitated through orderly mechanisms such as SSR (sustained silent reading), journals, reading and writing workshops, and of course, the version of literature circles described in this book. We can also allow for student direction amid true negotiated-inquiry projects— theme studies in which kids' agendas really rule.

On the other hand, in teacher-directed or -guided instruction, teachers design complex and sophisticated sequences of activities that lead kids into areas they wouldn't explore on their own, that model different kinds of thinking, that teach strategies and skills, that integrate the content areas of the curriculum. Yes, that may include teacher presentations—as veteran writers/readers, subject-area experts, skillful researchers, high-level thinkers, teachers can demonstrate their own thinking, sharing the path of their meaning making with students.

Does this mean teachers can still teach? You bet. Even though literature circles and many of the other key activities of holistic teaching occur during student-sponsored, independent time, we still need a balance. Notice that the list of key activities on pages 169–70 prominently features slots for *reading aloud, guided reading, and guided writing,* activities during which the teacher takes the lead, offering a planned, structured lesson that pursues a theme or teaches some content.

So there are still plenty of important opportunities for teachers to get up in front of thirty kids and lead, demonstrate, model, show, tell, instruct, share, present . . . heck, even *lecture.* But we now realize that such teaching episodes need to be both shorter and less frequent than they have traditionally been, so that we have time to balance them with the vital and neglected independent activities, with literature circles and the rest.

Scheduling for Balance

What does this balance look like in practice? Figure 9–1 is one example: a simplified version of Ruth Freedman's schedule for her second/third-grade room at the Baker Demonstration School at National-Louis University. Ruth's basic plan keeps kids' self-directed work time separate from her guided instruction by allocating about half the day to each.

Ruth's schedule is, of course, only one example of a teacher's careful balancing of guided and independent time. But it is a reminder that the ideal school day is *not* 100 percent theme studies, no matter how elegant and involving the unit might be. There should *always* be time saved for kids to choose and direct their own work. When students get older and see teachers only for short periods, then the time for independent work may have to *alternate* with teacher-guided thematic studies, occurring on alternate days or weeks, or in cycles. Admittedly, it's very hard for teachers to make these wholesale changes in their teaching schedule, devoting big new chunks of every school day or week to kids' self-sponsored learning, especially when there's that huge curriculum guide sitting on the shelf, mandating what we're supposed to "cover." And then we also struggle with our old, comfortable habits, our surefire lesson plans, and our potentially unmet ego needs.

Figure 9–1　Daily schedule for a second/third-grade class

Morning—Unit Work

8:30– 9:00	Opening Activities
9:00–11:00	Theme Work—extended thematic units that integrate math, science, social studies, research, with teacher-guided reading and writing
11:00–11:30	Specials (music, gym, etc.)
11:30–12:30	Lunch & Recess

Afternoon—Student-Directed Work

12:30–1:00	Specials (music, gym, etc.)
1:00–2:00	Writing Workshop
2:00–3:00	Literature Study Groups/Reading Workshop
3:00–3:10	Closing Activities

In our 1993 book *Best Practice: New Standards for Teaching and Learning in America's Schools,* Steve Zemelman, Art Hyde, and I wrote at some length on the subject of teachers' hunger to teach the old way. Since I'm very unlikely to improve upon what we wrote then, I'll close with a quote from that chapter:

> All of the [recommended] activities have one thing in common: they take the teacher off stage. They do not cast the teacher in the familiar role of information-dispenser, font-of-wisdom, expert/presenter/lecturer. In each of these key classroom structures, the teacher is somewhere further in the background, acting as a moderator, facilitator, coach, scribe, designer, observer, model—everything *but* the standard, normal, stereotypical, conception of the teacher as . . . well, as a *teacher.* What gives? Does this mean that in the idealized, progressive Best Practice classroom the teacher never "teaches" in the old-fashioned sense of the word?
>
> Not at all. But once again, balance is the key. It is fine for teachers to conduct whole-class presentations, to give information, to share and tell and even lecture—*some of the time.* But time-sharing is the key. In the traditional curriculum, we have catastrophically neglected

the student-centered side of the "airtime" equation. Indeed, one of the key findings from classroom research across subjects is that students don't get enough time to try out, practice, and apply what teachers are talking about. Kids never get to do any science or any writing or any math, because the teacher is so busy *talking* that there is never any time to practice the target activity.

Because it is so deeply ingrained in our culture that teaching means talking at other people who are silent and inactive, we all must police ourselves very closely to make sure we don't regress to that old transmission model. That's one reason why this chapter may seem so unbalanced, giving almost all of its attention to the structures for student-centered classroom time. But teachers already know how to conduct whole-class presentations, probably all too well. It was highlighted in their professional training, it was the core of their personal experience as students, and it probably predominates in their on-the-job experience. Most American teachers simply don't need as much help conducting whole-class presentations as they do with, for example, facilitating a [literature circle or] collaborative workshop. So teachers need to fill this gap, to correct this imbalance in their professional repertoire by equipping themselves with all the classroom structures they need to comfortably and safely get off stage, to provide and manage plenty of kid-centered time for practice and exploration. . . .

When we talk about balancing between teacher-directed and student-centered activities, it always boils down to how *time* is spent. Teachers must design days, weeks, years that provide kids a rich alternation between different configurations, groupings, and activities. The schedule must be predictable so students can prepare, mentally and even unconsciously, for what is coming up. . . . The balance in a day's or week's activities must also include things that make teachers reasonably comfortable, and yet teachers need to be growing and challenging themselves, too. In the end, school is more satisfying when everyone is growing and stretching themselves every day.

To work toward the goal of Best Practice, to embody the changes recommended [in this book], most teachers need to enrich their classroom repertoire in two directions: 1) setting aside time and building classroom structures that support more *student-directed activity,* using the . . . key structures outlined in the past few pages; and 2) making their *teacher-directed* activities both less predominant and more effective. We've seen that when teachers learn practical strategies to manage both of these modes of instruction, the curricular improvements they desire begin to take hold.

CHAPTER TEN

Problems, Questions, and Variations

T HE QUESTIONS addressed below are the ones most often asked in workshops and the ones that were most consistently raised in a survey we conducted of about fifty teachers who use literature circles. The answers offered here are mostly stolen from observations of *other* teachers, people who had faced the same difficulties and worked out their own creative solutions to these common problems.

A Warning: Plan to Trust the Kids

First, an opening note. The most prevalent problem that faces teachers as they try to implement literature circles is *patience*. In conversations and surveys, many teachers have confessed their tendency to worry, to expect too much too soon, to intervene prematurely, to rush in and take over, to lose faith in the kids and the process.

So here's the most important warning of all: wait. Don't panic. It will take hold in time. No educational change is ever instantaneous. Complex changes take even longer. If you really want to transfer responsibility and authority to your students, you are talking about a significant break with kids' past experience with school—and yours. Changes this large require some transition time, and you better be ready to live through it.

Indeed, when their patience starts to fail, truly progressive teachers—the real innovators—don't immediately complain about the kids. Instead, they start to question *themselves*. Not blame, mind you, but openly question. They wonder, Why am I so impatient? Am I getting itchy because, at heart, I really want to take over again? Maybe I miss being the center of attention and the source of control—presenting, telling, demanding, "really teaching."

Indeed, this "teacher ego problem" may be the unseen iceberg that has sunk thousands of instructional innovations. Many of us originally chose teaching as a career partly because of our need for personal display, for performing, for being the star of the show. So when we experiment with activities, like lit circles, that *take the teacher off stage,* we may feel deep ambivalence. Sometimes, if our own ego is not being satisfied, we may start finding reasons why a given student-centered innovation is "unworkable" or "unsuccessful," and needs to be dropped in favor of our return to center stage. As teachers, all we can do is be vigilant and self-critical, and steer around the ego iceberg. As far as literature circles are concerned, it is key to their success that teachers not dominate the process or the groups. The teacher must find personal gratification in the creation, facilitation, and support of the student-run discussions.

Questions and Concerns

1. Where am I supposed to get time *for literature circles? My schedule is already jam-packed with mandated activities as it is.*

In our literature circles network, we have promulgated The First Law of Curriculum Change, which goes like this: don't add anything to your teaching without subtracting something first. This law recognizes the one worst character flaw of most of us who teach. We will start with a schedule that uses 100 percent of our time with kids, and then we go and add something more to it. We end up doing 120 percent of what's possible—and feeling exhausted, fragmented, unappreciated, and stressed out. So the first answer to the time problem is: if you want to try lit circles, first find someplace in your schedule where you could, at least temporarily, remove an activity and clear away a regular chunk of time for a couple of weeks. In looking for that disposable ingredient of your curriculum, try to discard the activity that benefits kids least—skills seatwork, worksheets, or drill activities are likely targets. But remember also that while kids are learning to do literature circles, they are actually reading and discussing, which is certainly not a radical departure from the mandates of most official curriculums.

We mention "a couple of weeks" advisedly, because it is important to run lit circles regularly enough and long enough for students to get the rhythm, hit their stride, and internalize the procedures. Once this is accomplished, if time continues to be tight you can mothball lit circles for a while, giving their chunk of time over to another activity. Then, a few weeks later, you can bring lit circles back for another run—kids will usually jump right to it, remembering immediately how to operate. Some teachers call this pattern "cycles," and they put literature circles in rotation with other activities like reading or writing workshop. Be aware, though, that once you start using lit circles, neither you nor your kids will want to give them up.

2. My kids ask closed-ended, factual-recall questions. They have mechanical, pro forma conversations. They dutifully take turns, but there's no authentic conversational spark.

Oftentimes this problem simply reflects kids' experience in school. If they are accustomed to literature discussions that focus on convergent, right-answer questions, then that's what they will instinctively recreate in their lit circles. They may need more training, along the lines of the "careful" training model described in Chapter 3. Take a look at the way Barbara Dress teaches kids about "fat" versus "skinny" questions on page 54. Or put your strongest group into a fishbowl, to demonstrate for the rest. Or read a story together as a whole group, asking everyone to think up three fat, juicy, open-ended questions for discussion. Then use the kids' own strongest questions to demonstrate what kind of prompts spark natural conversation about literature. It may take some time for students to really believe in, and act out, your new model for them.

However, this problem can also indicate that true literature circles haven't been implemented. Perhaps the teacher is intruding or monitoring a bit too much. Maybe he is trying to infuse a good dose of "skills" into the circles. We're not saying that direct instruction is *evil*; but it should be saved for another time in the schedule. Now, during lit circles, we want to send congruent messages that kids are in control of their learning. So when groups are listless, we have to ask, Are kids reading books they have freely chosen? Are they meeting in groups they have freely entered? If kids are passive, dependent, and uncreative, it is sometimes because they are feeling *controlled* and are therefore being submissive.

3. My kids digress a lot. They're talking animatedly, but the conversation wanders pretty far from the book.

If you want to feel better about this problem right away, go and visit an adult reading group at your local community center or bookstore. You'll notice that veteran readers digress a great deal. Indeed, this can be one of the key signs of health in a literature circle—that kids use books as a springboard to discussing the big-value questions of life that literature, at its best, raises.

If you're still really worried, sit in with the troubled group for a full session. The design of the role sheets encourages kids to keep coming back to the text; they're invited to point out and talk about specific sections, passages, even words—so it takes some real effort, some serious inattention, or a transcendent digression to keep kids separated from the text for too long. If the conversation really isn't somehow centering on the book, then you can intervene. It's perfectly okay for a teacher to ask students, How is this conversation connected to the book? Many times they will be able to tell you. If they can't, then this opens the door to talking about keeping the book as the loose center of the conversation. Some lit circle teachers even have this motto emblazoned on a poster in their classrooms: TAKE IT BACK TO THE BOOK. This is a reminder to everyone that we are sharing and weighing ideas within, as Louise Rosenblatt so eloquently puts it, the gravitational field of the text.

4. What do you do about kids who are uninterested or unmotivated, or who misbehave in literature circles?

Sometimes teachers ask this question with the implication that student noncooperation with literature circles actually seems like a pretty reasonable response to this unusual activity. To those teachers, one answer is, Well, what would you do if you told your class, Please take out your science books, and one child absolutely refused to do it? Which is to say: your repertoire of strategies for dealing with misbehavior or inattention in literature circles is *exactly the same* as it is for any other instructional technique you might choose to employ. You have conferences with them, write them notes, talk to the parents, set up a points or rewards contract—whatever it takes to get the kid working effectively.

After all, in order to have a productive classroom, all teachers must find ways of enforcing their own standards of engagement. And while they operate with empathy and sensitivity, committed teachers do enforce those standards. Just as it is *not okay* by most of our standards for a kid continually to refuse to do any science, it is similarly *not okay* for him to misbehave in or undermine his literature circle.

On a brighter note, I find that lit circles are often the *answer,* not the problem, for kids who are disaffected, marginalized, or unsuccessful in school. This structure offers a chance to be active, to do something, to make some choices, to interact with peers, to get some positive attention. While the transition to literature circles may be especially bumpy for kids on the margins, the final payoff is often greatest for them.

5. How do you handle lower-ability or special education kids in literature circles?

As we discussed in Chapter 2, literature circles are one of the most powerful natural structures for heterogeneous grouping. Including "low-ability" students should not present any problem in real literature circles—in fact, it's a plus. The varied experiences and perspectives brought to book discussions by kids of different backgrounds are *assets*. Further, the diverse learning styles accessed by the role sheets allow all kinds of kids to shine in discussion, at least on some days.

When they are working well, kids pick books—and work in discussion groups—that are generally at their own level. However, the possibility to move up or down the scale of difficulty, work with different kids, see other skills and interests modeled, is always there. And, because the teacher isn't making whole-class presentations, she is available to help.

Most kids who are labeled as learning disabled or special ed are actually able to do just fine with higher-order thinking—for many, it is the lower-order operations (like decoding text on a page) that gives them trouble in school. If these kids can just get the book or the story into their heads, then they have tons to say, as much as anybody, about feelings, events, values, ideas, conflict, people. So when special education students select books for their literature circles that are simply too hard for them to plow through fluently, teachers provide help. They make sure that someone—an aide, parent, peer, or consulting special education teacher—is available to read the book aloud or that the book is available on audiotape in the classroom. If a literature circle group contains several kids who have picked a book above their fluency level, then the whole group may use read-alouds or audiotapes to make sure they get into and understand the story. When teachers provide these kinds of assistance, they ensure that *all* kids get to experience the essence of literature circles, which is not decoding but discussing the ideas in and around books.

6. Won't the top children be shortchanged in literature circles?

Gifted and talented kids are an important part of a rich literature circle mix. On a day-to-day basis, since free choice of books is a hallmark of LCs, these kids will probably be reading thick, challenging books and discussing them in the company of some other "gifted children." But if the circles are really working right, the groups won't be segregated; they'll often shift, and the partners won't always be other certified "giftees." Instead, some group members will be other sorts of kids—either because those kids have "picked up" to a harder book or because the gifted child has "picked down" to an easier book.

When this happens, literature circles are serving gifted kids very well. Often, children in this category have one or two highly developed areas of excellence—art, music, language, or math. But they may be greatly lacking in the street smarts, physical awareness, cultural knowledge, people sense, or emotional maturity that some other, so-called low-level kids enjoy. Truly, when the subject is literature and the task is discussion, diversity is a benefit to everyone.

By the way, if "gifted parents" are your real concern, here's a rejoinder that seems to elicit their support for literature circles: Well, would you rather have us go back to the old way, where the whole class reads the same book, pitched at the average readers in the group?

7. What about shy kids who don't like group activities?

Just as with special education, low-achieving, and other kids who struggle in school, literature circles should be one of the solutions—not another problem—for quiet children. This structure offers shy kids a chance to speak up and be heard, not in the scary arena of the whole class, but in a three- to five-member group whose friendship, hopefully, feels more solid and safe as days go by. The informality, the predictable structure, the low-stress atmosphere, the absence of right-answer pressure, and the welcoming of differences—all these features of lit circles help to encourage risk taking by kids who are tentative.

Always, of course, teachers must balance the potential of an activity like literature circles to "bring out" a shy kid with that child's right to be shy. If viewed as a learning-style issue, perhaps shyness shouldn't be "treated" or "overcome," but simply respected and accommodated. Thus, some caring teachers may decide, after giving literature circles every opportunity to invite a shy child in, that it's okay for one or two such kids to pursue their independent reading alone or in pairs, while most others work in groups. This is one of the toughest, sometimes heart-wrenching choices that professional teachers make.

8. What about students who come to their circles unprepared?

Most of the answer to this question can be found under Question 1. While literature circles offer kids a tremendous amount of freedom, choice, and creativity, they are also a serious school assignment. It is congruent, therefore, for teachers consistently to enforce reasonable standards of engagement. It is a real loss for the individual child to neglect reading or preparing for literature circle meetings. It is also a disservice to the group, which depends for its success on the participation of every member.

In practice, the kids in the groups tend to take care of this problem. Many teachers have testified that once the circles are established and valued, kids vigorously police each other. As teacher Kristen Overcash reports: "They're kind and thoughtful unless someone comes to the circle unprepared—in which case they're harder on one another than I ever am on them."

If the reluctant or unmotivated students are highly grade-oriented, some teachers will set up a point system in the early days of literature circles. Typically, they'll give kids ten points for arriving prepared for each lit circle meeting, meaning they've read the assignment and have their role sheet or reading log filled out. This approach works best when the points are over and above regular class work—free or bonus points—and awarded strictly on a checkoff, all-or-nothing basis. You don't want to be arguing with a kid about what's a seven and what's a six while you are trying to get literature circles to work. Whatever point system is devised, it's best to phase it out just as soon as students will read for the pleasure of the literature and the conversations.

9. What do you do when students are absent from a group? When they return?

Sandy King has a nice way of handling missing members of literature circles in her third-grade classroom. She has a menagerie of stuffed animals, and she puts one in the seat of any absent child. On many a day, Paddington Bear has served as passage master or word wizard for a group! Sandy's message to the children, of course, is, You can do just fine with the members who are left. If the absent child happens to be the discussion director, the teacher may have to designate a new chairperson/convener for the group and make sure kids can generate good discussion questions from the passages, drawings, and vocabulary brought by the members who are present. But there is also an intentional redundancy in the design of role sets for readers of all ages—you can have fine discussions based on any two or three roles. Indeed, this is often what happens even when all group members are present; a "hot topic" gets launched by one or two contributions, and none of the other notes or roles is needed to keep the conversation going. Needless to say, in a group where kids have already "graduated" from role sheets, the remaining group members will do fine using their reading logs.

For the student who misses a session, literature circles are a relatively easy assignment to make up. Obviously, the child has to catch up on the reading, and should do the missing role sheets, turning them in to the group or teacher, as appropriate. When the absent kid returns, it is a valuable exercise—for everyone—for the group to offer the returning member a summary of the missed discussions; students may refer to previous day's role sheets to cue their memory about this.

10. What happens when kids pick books that are too hard for them? too easy? Does the teacher continue to let kids make bad choices?

Literature circles are designed to be essentially self-leveling, and few teachers report finding kids who repeatedly pick books they cannot read. The only recurrent pattern is children who pick their books solely to place themselves into a certain circle of kids regardless of their own real reading tastes or abilities. That, of course, becomes the subject of one-to-one conversation and guidance. The teacher may need to have the student try reading a bit of the chosen book in a conference, which will probably make any comprehension problems very plain. Then the two can talk about selecting another, more accessible book—perhaps in the same genre—next time.

On the other hand, the very structure of literature circles is meant to invite kids occasionally to try a harder-than-usual book. When a kid does pick a book that's above his current fluency level, teachers should first of all celebrate: what a nice opportunity and incidence of positive risk taking! Next, the teacher can help the child succeed by making sure he internalizes the book somehow. This may mean having an aide, peer helper, or parent read all or parts of the book aloud—or getting the book on tape so the student can listen to it as he reads. With this help, the kid will get enough of the story to be a valuable member of later literature circle conversations.

Students in lit circle classrooms do sometimes get into below-level reading "ruts," selecting, say, one *Babysitters' Club* title after another. This phenomenon tends to co-occur with the problem behind Question 11 below—groups that don't reshuffle often. When this syndrome occurs, teachers start by asking themselves, Well, haven't *I* ever gotten stuck on one genre of "beach books" or one author—reading a whole string of mysteries or gothic romances in a row? Readers do enjoy plateauing with a beloved genre—indeed, that's often what we mean by "pleasure reading."

If a teacher is still concerned, she can use a variety of strategies to give the kid a nudge. She can write a dialogue journal note to the stuck student, suggesting other titles. She can conduct a book selection conference, giving the student a quick, tantalizing summary of four or five non–*Babysitters' Club* titles. If the teacher has set up a classroom evaluation system that gives points for range, breadth, or risk taking in reading, a reminder of this fact might be a nice bit of iron-fist-in-a-velvet-glove guidance.

11. Every time we select new books, my kids always end up in the same group with the same friends—how can I ensure some mixing?

The reason for this might simply be that your groups are finishing at different times and there are no others available to re-form with. That's one reason why many successful lit circle teachers establish *ending dates* for each cycle, guaranteeing that everyone is potentially available when new groups get formed. If your kids still act clannish, the first recourse is to talk about this problem with them openly, reminding them that one of the best features of lit circles is variety, in both books and discussion partners.

If reasoning doesn't work, blind voting probably will. Next time kids finish a cycle and it's time to pick new books, have them turn in a prioritized ballot of three or four choices for their next book. In order to ensure this will work, you should do this unannounced, so kids don't have a chance to conspire on the playground to pick the same book/group again. Then you can take the lists and compose the groups privately, with reshuffling a high priority. Who knows? You might give a kid their third or fourth choice for the sole reason of forming a new, promising group. That's some real *facilitation*.

12. What if kids pick a book I haven't read?

Great! There's much to be learned when a child is reading a book *we* don't know. Then we can honestly and congruently ask, What's it about? Why did she do that? What do you think will happen next? In fact, many teachers find that when they haven't read a book, they can be more probing with kids.

It works the other way around, too. If the teacher decides to read the book and join a group as a fellow reader, she can do some wonderful teaching. After all, as Robert Probst (1988) reminds us, one of the best experiences kids can have is seeing a teacher read a book for the very first time, enjoying a close-up demonstration of how a mature reader makes predictions, constructs meaning, and connects with a book. It's important that book recommendations flow *both ways* in the classroom—that teachers get turned on to books by students, just as much as they recommend their favorites to the kids. If you are worried about the appropriateness of kids' book choices, see the next item.

13. What about books with questionable content—ones with sex, violence, racism, or rough language?

Some of our literature circle network teachers have solved this problem skillfully. Where the main concern is edgy parents, they simply use a bland permission letter saying, "Your child has selected this book to read in a literature circle beginning next week. You may want to read it also. Please let me know if you have any comments." There's a place for the parent to sign off that they have reviewed the book. Once parents have said okay, teachers and kids are free to proceed. If the parent objects, the kid picks another book.

Sometimes teachers themselves are disturbed by the book choices kids make, even with the informed approval of their parents. They object to the graphic horror of Steven King, the formulaic repetition of the *Hardy Boys,* the degrading female stereotypes in the *Babysitters' Club* books. When it is the teacher's turn to assign books to the whole class—which most of us still do during other parts of the school day—then we are free to demonstrate our literary standards and, ideally, to explain them. But the purpose of literature circles is to build fluency and a love of reading by choosing one's own books—and that right should not be gratuitously abridged by the tastes of others, even the teacher. That means we bite our tongue and let kids choose.

14. Can I start my literature circles without using the role sheets? They seem kind of contrived and artificial.

Sure, you can try it. In solid, well-established whole language classrooms, kids may be completely ready to run their own searching, productive discussions. But unless your kids are already pretty experienced with such group work, omitting the roles may lead to this: the kids will talk, perhaps even vigorously, but their conversation will "orbit" quite far from the book they are reading. Typically, someone will throw out an initial idea or association derived from the reading, and then the group will be off on twenty or thirty minutes of free associations. The conversation may be stimulating and vigorous. It just won't be a literature circle, because the book has been left in the dust.

The role sheets *are* artificial and contrived. They were purposely "contrived," among other things, to help students keep their heads rooted in the book, to keep coming back, over and over again, to look at what an author has said. Once kids have used the sheets long enough to internalize this habit of mind, they toss the sheets away and continue on their own. But they always "Bring it back to the book." In general, groups that haven't first used the roles for a while never develop this habit.

As we've also stressed throughout the book, the role sheets are supposed to be a temporary training device, not a permanent classroom fixture, so if you feel uncomfortable with these sheets, remember they won't be around long. Some teachers, like Sally Ryan at Baker Demonstration School, teach the kids the roles in whole-class sessions, using the sheets only to make the different tasks clear. Then, when kids are really reading a book for their lit circle, they do their note writing in reading logs. That means the kids never fill out any worksheet–like pages, but they do use the sheets for training in the roles and in discussing.

15. *What about all the noise literature circles seem to create?*

One anonymous sixth-grade teacher in our survey had a great answer to this question: "Noise!" she wrote. "The voices of excited kids carry very far. They do get excited. I *want* them to be excited!" And she's right. Noise is almost a barometer of kids' engagement in literature circles: if it's loud, it's probably working.

Noise is really only a problem if one of three conditions exists: (1) The kids can't hear one another well enough to work. (2) The teacher is going crazy. (3) People outside the classroom, like other teachers in the corridor or the principal, are annoyed. All three problems need to be solved, and all have the same solution: "the twelve-inch voice." Here's how our colleague Barbara Dress solves this problem. She tells kids that they have been using their "ten-foot (or three-mile!) voices" and need to grow a "twelve-inch voice." She has them practice adjusting their volume so they are inaudible from the next literature circle. She even has intermediate-grade kids kneel on their desk chairs so their faces are brought together and they do literally talk at a one-foot distance and keep their voices down. In Sandy King's room, where Barbara trained the students, the official command that now starts literature circles is "Butts Up!"—for obvious reasons.

16. How can one teacher answer all those reading logs?

First of all, reading logs are supposed to be writing-to-learn, which means that their main purpose is to help the writer think, not to entertain an audience. In literature circles, the logs usually replace the role sheets as a place for kids to reflect on their reading and jot notes for the next discussion. So the logs are not, by nature, writing for an audience.

Yet if your kids *do* really hunger for input from you, what do you do? Read only five logs per day. Try not to take them home, but read them during SSR time. Give short responses on *small* Post-it notes. Have kids turn in only a fraction of the logs they write—have them pick the one entry per week they most want to share with you. If you're compulsive, you can scan them all, but answer just one. Or set up (and train) kid partners for dialogue journals—why should *you* be the bottleneck through which all work passes, anyway?

17. How can I get more skills instruction into my literature circles?

Literature circles *do* teach reading skills. They teach about the nature of different genres, about authors' craft with words, about ways characters reveal themselves, and a thousand other valuable skills. Every time a literature circle meets, multiple skills are being practiced, reinforced, or strengthened. However, skills are being learned *implicitly*, through practice and use, not *explicitly*, through teacher presentation. And the particular skills addressed will be *different for every child every day*, and the *sequence will be completely unpredictable*.

To do literature circles is to affirm a belief in incidental learning, in learning by doing, in scaffolded interaction. That's why teachers set aside this one special time of day for kids to just read and just talk, running their own learning. Teachers still control the rest of the day's schedule, and they can conduct skill lessons then. What most teachers find, though, is that the learning from real reading and talking is much stronger than from directed instruction, and they reallocate more and more time away from teacher presentations and into literature circles, workshops, and other student-directed structures.

> **18. Can I use literature circles to teach a single required book? or sets of required books or readings? How about required nonfiction materials in content areas? Can I use circles to teach my integrated, thematic units?**

Of course. Since we've already repeatedly had our say about the importance of student choice, we won't reiterate it here. As long as kids' school experience is well balanced and they are having plenty of student-directed time elsewhere in their day, in other structures like workshops or journals or negotiated-inquiry projects, then it's fine to harness literature circles to a bit of prescribed curriculum. That's exactly what Donna Stupple (Chapter 7) and Debbie O'Connor (Chapter 6) have done in their classrooms.

If the choice is between studying a book in literature circles or in a whole-class lecture-discussion, then literature circles offer a much better format. They allow for active participation by everyone at once, rather than the laborious turn taking and passive turn waiting of the large-group approach. The small-group format also invites kids' real questions into the mix and safeguards against teacher domination of all conversations. Indeed, once teachers have tried using the "basic" literature circles model—where kids pick their own books—they often prefer to use this structure, rather than the older, teacher-centered approaches, for *all* literature study. This is how the influence of literature circles begins to reach out across the entire school program, transforming everything—giving students more voice and more choice all day long.

Literature circles can also be used to teach required authors, genres, or other sets of texts. Curriculum guides don't always prescribe the exact books to be read; sometimes they just want certain types of materials to be covered. So if your kids are mandated to read, for example, a Shakespeare play, a book on insects, a Roald Dahl novel, a Hemingway story, a research report on nuclear energy, or a canto of *Paradise Lost,* you can offer them several of each to choose from. Then, you can use the lit circles roles and structures to facilitate a more student-centered discussion.

This procedure, which brings a degree of student choice and voice even to very official school activities, is closely akin to the structure called "text sets," which was devised by Kathy Short (Harste, Short, and Burke 1988). This procedure is especially attractive to teachers of science, social studies, and other "content-area" fields. Rather than requiring, for example, that each student in a history class read superficially through the accounts of all Civil War battles, kids can join literature circles that pick just one battle from a "text set" of battle accounts to read and discuss. Later, the groups can connect in a wider discussion, jigsawing their articles and looking for similarities and differences in the individual battles.

19. Can you have literature circles where each member reads something different, instead of everyone reading the same text?

This is exactly how a lot of primary—especially kindergarten—teachers operate their literature circles as a matter of routine (see Chapter 6). It's also a variant of the strategy of "text sets" we just looked at above. When each member of a small discussion group has read something different, the discussion procedures obviously need to be adjusted. Each member has to introduce and summarize their reading first, and perhaps answer any questions, before wider sharing and comparing can go on. When such heterogeneous groups meet to discuss the reading of individually selected literature, it typically becomes a sharing and "advertising" session, in which kids savor or pan books they have read and answer questions from their peers. Such meetings don't do much to support reading in process (nor to question or push anyone's thinking), and so they usually happen only after books are completed.

Heterogeneous literature circles seem to work better when they are based on some kind of "text set"—materials related by topic, genre, author, or some other point of similarity. Then each group member has more to do than wait her or his turn. If we are all reading mysteries, then there are genuinely common features and overlaps to be listened for, noted, and explored, and the conversation can become cumulative. The nonfiction and jigsaw role sheets on pages 103 and 104 are designed to help orchestrate just these kinds of heterogeneous literature circle meetings.

One of our favorite activities with older kids and teachers is the "homogeneous-heterogeneous swap," which is based on a topical text set. (We often use a group of articles about changing gender roles.) Readers begin in a group where everyone has read the same article. Here, there are two stages of discussion—first, people just talk, having that good old-fashioned lit circle natural conversation about the text. Then, in the last five minutes, we ask them to come up with a "consensus highlight" from their reading— one aspect or idea that everyone agrees ought to be shared with people who haven't read this article. They talk this out and each member jots down notes or key words from the agreed-on highlight. Then everyone swaps, finding their way into a new group where everyone has read a different article in the text set. This meeting begins with a round, in which each circle member tells the title and author of his or her article and then shares the consensus highlight developed in the homogeneous group. General conversation then follows. This is the most concrete demonstration of curriculum jigsawing we've found: everyone learns a lot about one topic and gets a taste of some closely related content without having to "cover" everything.

20. Is it okay to teach in a literature circle? Can't I join a group as a more active instructor, not just as a facilitator or fellow reader? I want to help kids read more intensively and deeply. Can't I do some of my guided instruction within the literature circles meetings?

Once you have the baseline, "original," student-directed version of literature circles operating, many valuable and interesting variations present themselves. The most immediate and instinctive one for many teachers is to add themselves to a group in a bit more directive role. This is the model that Karen Smith evolved in her Arizona classroom and that we described on page 67. Her student book groups would meet with just kids three out of four weeks, and then about one week a month with her. When Karen was a group member, she didn't just sit back as a fellow reader, but took an active role in helping students note and understand ideas, themes, and elements of the author's craft.

Karen and the group of kids she was going to meet with always picked the book together, mutually. After everyone read the book, they'd gather a first time just to talk: "Our first meeting often consists of a lot of personal responses," Karen explains. "We talk about people, events, or other books we were reminded of. We share parts of the story we didn't understand. We point out exceptionally powerful writing and discuss the author's techniques." Toward the end of this first session, the group, together, identifies some focus for discussion over the next few days. "Sometimes we retrace a character's journey, marking those events that seemed significant in his or her development. Sometimes we mark events that reveal characters' relationships. Sometimes we reread with point of view in mind. Each time we turn back to the text to enrich our current understandings" (in Short and Pierce

1990, p. 22). Karen's literature groups model, obviously, reflects thoughtful, balanced, elegant teaching.

On the other hand, literature circles can very easily become a delivery system for old-fashioned teacher-centered instruction. When groups only meet one at a time and always with the teacher running the group, the meetings look and feel and sound very much like an old-fashioned three-group basal reading program. Unfortunately, such tendencies are inadvertently stoked when teacher leadership of small-group discussions is added to the literature circles model as if it were a minor variation.

We'll say it one last time: student-led discussion is the main value and defining attribute of literature circles. Unsatisfied teacher egos can lead to the corruption of almost any student-centered design. We teachers must police *ourselves* by creating balanced schedules that authentically share the day between our "airtime" and kids' inquiry and practice. Otherwise, even though it may be inadvertent and unconscious, we may subtly transform literature circles into yet another chunk of teacher-dominated time.

21. I keep forgetting to evaluate my kids' literature circles—what should I do?

First of all, *why* are you forgetting to evaluate? Is it because you're so absorbed by the process, so knocked out by what the kids are saying, so caught up in your own reading of kids' literature? This is what keeps happening to Marianne Flanagan, one of the teachers whose stories open this book. Periodically, she resolves to do some evaluation, to get around to each group, to take some notes, to write up kids' participation. But what usually happens is that she sits down in the first group, immediately gets drawn into the conversation, and becomes so involved with the kids and the ideas at hand that the whole period goes by. Marianne doesn't even get to another group, much less evaluate anyone.

Of course, what has happened is far more valuable. Marianne has given an authentic, heartful, extended demonstration of adult reading and thinking to the kids in one group. In other words, she has been *teaching*. But also, if you ask her later about the individual kids in that group, she can talk in elaborate detail about how everyone is doing, what chapter they're on, what they think of the book, what they've read before, what kids they work with best, what kinds of questions interest them, and all the rest. So she *is* assessing children all the time, using *teacher observation and judgment*—but she evaluates not as an outside judge but as a side-by-side participant-observer. Most of Marianne's evaluation activities are not definably separate from her teaching—and her teaching is always, in part, evaluative.

If Marianne or any other teacher wants or needs to take the final step, making the outcomes of this teacher observation visible and official, she can implement a few of the six evaluation strategies outlined in Chapter 8.

CHAPTER ELEVEN

• • • • • • • •

Teaching Teachers about Literature Circles

I N   O R D E R to tap the power and potential of literature circles for their own classrooms, teachers need to experience the activity for themselves. The following workshop/demonstration, designed to introduce teachers to literature circles, uses the 1990 Newbery Medal–winning novel *Maniac Magee,* by Jerry Spinelli. As befits a group of adults, this workshop is designed to plunge people pretty quickly into literature circles; it introduces a full set of different roles on the first try rather than spacing out the training over several days, as we might do in a classroom of children. The workshop is presented in the form of directions for the group facilitator:

1. *Read aloud:* Read the prologue, "Before the Story," from *Maniac Magee.* (With a different book, this could be the first chapter, the introduction, or some involving sample of the text.)
2. *Respond:* Invite pairs of participants to talk for two minutes about any reactions or responses they had to this read-aloud. Stress open, personal response.
3. *Share:* Ask a few people to share a highlight or thread of their conversation.
4. *Explain:* Briefly talk about the concept of LCs: mention that it melds a reader response approach with cooperative learning.
5. *Form groups:* Divide the participants into groups of four or five each and make sure everyone knows what group they're in.
6. *Hand out roles:* Distribute copies of the role sheets to each group. (Have them precollated and ready to go. As you hand them out, you need to be sure who is in which group.)
7. *Clarify roles:* Have one volunteer for each role read aloud the description of that role. Make any clarifying or elaborating comments

that will help. (This way everyone knows what other roles will be played in the group.)

8. *Give assignment:* "Read Chapters 1 to 5 with your role in mind, putting the appropriate notes on your sheet while and after you read. If you get ahead of others, please don't read ahead, but rather jot personal responses or possible group discussion topics on the back of your sheet. When we reconvene in about fifteen minutes, please be ready to play your role in your group's discussion."

9. *Explain:* As you send groups off to meet, stress that the discussion director is the convener. It is her or his job to make sure everyone gets some "airtime" to play their prepared role, as well as to simply share ideas. The goal is a *natural conversation* about the content of the reading, with people offering their role contribution wherever it fits. If people don't volunteer, the DD should gently solicit their input. Announce the time available.

10. *Groups meet* (about 15–20 minutes): Visit the groups, gently and unobtrusively, to note how people are functioning and to provide help if needed.

11. *Reassemble the whole group and debrief:* Start with some talk about *the content of the reading,* about people's responses to the book. Then debrief the *strategy,* the roles, the activity, talking about ways this structure could be adapted to the different grade levels and curriculum concerns of the teachers in the group.

Follow-up

One of the remarkable things about literature circles is that they are so simple. While many of the other key activities in progressive, whole language classrooms, such as writing workshops or thematic units, are exquisitely complex and can take much effort to get going, literature circles are different. Though there are, of course, a thousand things that can go wrong (or right) with the activity, the basic, underlying structure is perfectly straightforward. That's why one quick introduction to the activity—in a workshop like the one above—is often enough to jump-start brave teachers like Marianne Flanagan and Marline Pearson. These innovative teachers go to an inservice session, read an article or two, prepare some role sheets, and *just do it.* And these pathfinders very often get literature circles 90 percent "right" the first time out.

Once teachers get excited about trying literature circles in their own classrooms, they can benefit from lots of support. Northbrook District 27, under the leadership of Curriculum Director Barbara Unikel, made a long-term commitment to implementing literature circles. First they supported an initial inservice program to get literature circles started in the classrooms of a dozen teachers who volunteered to try them. Then they sent a few of the most enthusiastic converts for summer leadership training at the Wal-loon Institute in northern Michigan. The following year, Northbrook offered interested faculty a *fourteen-session workshop* to help them plan and debrief their own classroom experiments with literature circles and related activities. Eight of these sessions were co-facilitated by an outside consultant and an in-district teacher-leader; the other six meetings were led by a local teacher-consultant alone. This extensive support system resulted in a very high level of implementation of literature circles. Today, literature circles are happening in the *majority* of classrooms in the district, and many of the best ideas in this book have been borrowed from those outstanding Northbrook teachers.

One Teacher's "Self-Inservice"

But even when the staff development program isn't optimal, literature circles can take hold anyhow. All that's required is a brave, caring teacher and a clear explanation. Marianne Flanagan, the Chicago fifth-grade teacher whose ideas appear throughout this book, started her literature circles on the basis of a five-minute conversation with a colleague and a set of hand-outs. Indeed, one of the things that makes Marianne such an effective teacher, especially in a setting where one could think of plenty excuses, is that she loves to experiment. Marianne is willing to try any promising idea, and she doesn't worry about preplanning an innovation to the last detail. She's secure in herself, and doesn't obsess about what might go wrong. She just tries things first and then fixes up the weak spots later. She doesn't expect perfection of herself or her kids. She knows that for kids and teachers alike, growth comes through taking risks and making mistakes.

Some teachers have gotten their lit circles going with even less input, guidance, and support than Marianne had. Here's a letter our network received from a Chicago Public School teacher, someone we'd never met or talked to and who had never attended any sort of "live" training. In fact, Charlotte's entire exposure to literature circles consisted of reading a couple of articles written by Marianne Flanagan, Jackie McWilliams, and other literature circle veterans and published in a local teacher newspaper.

Dear Colleagues,

I am a fourth-grade teacher at Clinton School in Chicago. I teach a self-contained classroom, and the only time during the day that my students move to another classroom is to go to their reading class.

Last school year (1991–1992) I decided to try literature circles in my reading class. This class was composed of above-grade-level readers, and I thought the circles would be a challenge for them to read more, and would also give them an opportunity to use their leadership and social skills. This group always had a *lot* to say.

In general, I felt that the concept of literature circles would give the class more control over learning. I wanted to put more responsibility on the student, instead of having my classroom stay teacher-directed as it had been in the past. I had only been teaching for five years, but I was ready for something different in my classroom. I wanted the reading class to be more exciting and relevant to the kids. And most of all, I wanted to see them really enjoy reading! So many of them had the idea that reading is a subject where they spend their time answering comprehension and workbook questions.

I have continued literature circles this school year because I was so pleased with what I experienced for my class last year.

I now have about fifteen titles, and I have grouped the students four to a group with a total of seven groups. I have used the role sheets, and the students each receive a new one, depending on their job, each time they meet. The grouping of the students is done by me, and the first book read by the groups was selected by me. After reading the first book, I then let the group pick which title it would like to read from then on.

It is very important to me to circulate around the room while the groups are discussing the books. When a book is finished, I conference with them on their feelings about the book, what they liked or didn't like about it, the message of what the book is saying, and how they would rate it on a scale of one to ten.

There are problems which arise from time to time. First, this is something very new to most kids. None of my students has ever done anything like this before. I always tell them that the group rises or falls because of each individual member. Sometimes they spend more time arguing over jobs or number of pages to be read than discussing the book. Problems arise when a student is absent, unprepared, or transfers to another school. I also worry about the kids losing the books, because I have been buying them myself, and some were received from a grant.

Despite the problems, I think the positive aspects far override the negative. When I circulate the room and sit with each group for a few minutes, I can see the benefits of this reading technique. By far the greatest advantage comes from the fact that the students are learning from each other. I always tell them that what you feel about a book may be different from another person, but it is fun to compare, discuss, react, and critique. When I hear them using words like theme, climax, etc., and then go on to discuss them in the books they are reading, I am elated. I have so much fun listening to them, and sometimes I will sit with one group and enter into the discussion. They can now compare characters well, and they now look for how a character changes in the story and solves his or her problem. It is very gratifying to me to see them doing this automatically.

As to my overall feelings, just writing about this has brought back memories of what has happened to my students because of literature circles. I think it would be very difficult for me *not* to do them every year. I wonder if I would be able to do them with a less motivated class composed of poor readers.

I would think that it would be very helpful to teachers if a workshop or inservice could be planned with literature circles as the topic. It would be wonderful to talk to other teachers about how they are using them in their classrooms, and how to expand on the ideas that have been written up to this point.

This letter turned out to be much longer than I planned. I get very excited about teaching reading, because I have always enjoyed reading myself. Literature circles have added much to the enjoyment I get from my reading class.

     Charlotte Ortiz

• • • • • • • • •

References

Allington, Richard. 1983. "The Reading Instruction Provided Readers of Differing Reading Abilities." *Elementary School Journal* (May).

Anderson, Richard, Elfrieda Hiebert, Judith Scott, and Ian Wilkerson. 1985. *Becoming a Nation of Readers.* Washington, DC: National Institute of Education.

Anderson, Richard, P. T. Wilson, and L. G. Fielding. 1988. "Growth in Reading and How Children Spend Their Time Outside of School." *Reading Research Quarterly* (Summer).

Applebee, Arthur. 1981. *Writing in the Secondary School: English and the Content Areas.* NCTE Research Report #21. Urbana, IL: National Council of Teachers of English.

Atwell, Nancie. 1987. *In the Middle: Writing, Reading, and Learning with Adolescents.* Portsmouth, NH: Boynton/Cook.

Beane, James. 1991. "Middle School: The Natural Home of Integrated Curriculum." *Educational Leadership* (October).

Bruner, Jerome, 1961. *The Process of Education.* Cambridge, MA: Harvard University Press.

Calkins, Lucy. 1986. *The Art of Teaching Writing.* Portsmouth, NH: Heinemann.

Close, Elizabeth Egan. 1992. "Literature Discussion: A Classroom Environment for Thinking and Sharing." *English Journal* (September).

Daniels, Harvey, and Steven Zemelman. 1985. *A Writing Project: Training Teachers of Composition from Kindergarten Through College.* Portsmouth, NH: Heinemann.

Dewey, John. 1916. *Democracy and Education.* New York: Macmillan.

Edelsky, Carole, Bess Altwerger, and Barbara Flores. 1990. *Whole Language: What's the Difference?* Portsmouth, NH: Heinemann.

Fader, Daniel. 1976. *The New Hooked on Books.* New York: Berkley.

Fielding, Leslie, and David Pearson. 1994. "Reading Comprehension: What Works." *Educational Leadership* (February).

Glasser, William. 1990. *The Quality School.* New York: Harper.

Goodman, Kenneth. 1986. *What's Whole in Whole Language?* Portsmouth, NH: Heinemann.

Harste, Jerome, Kathy Short, and Carolyn Burke. 1988. *Creating Classrooms for Authors: The Reading-Writing Connection.* Portsmouth, NH: Heinemann.

Harwayne, Shelley. 1992. *Lasting Impressions: Weaving Literature into the Writing Workshop.* Portsmouth, NH: Heinemann.

Heath, Shirley Brice. 1985. *Ways with Words: Language, Life and Work in Communities and Classrooms.* New York: Cambridge University Press.

Heath, Shirley Brice, and Leslie Mangiola. 1991. *Children of Promise: Literate Activity in Linguistically and Culturally Diverse Classrooms.* Washington, DC: National Education Association.

Johnson, David, Roger Johnson, Edythe Holubec, and Patricia Roy. 1991. *Cooperation in the Classroom.* Edina, MN: Interaction Book Company.

Keegan, Suzi, and Karen Shrake. 1991. "Literature Study Groups: An Alternative to Ability Grouping." *Reading Teacher* (April).

Kohn, Alfie. 1993. "Choices for Children: Why and How to Let Students Decide." *Phi Delta Kappan* (October).

Kroll, Marianne, and Ann Paziotopoulos. 1992. *Literature Circles: Practical Ideas and Strategies for Responding to Literature.* Darien, IL: M. Kroll. Available from M. Kroll, 1717 Lakeview Drive, Darien, IL 60561.

———. 1993. *Mark It: Theme Bookmarks and Other Activities for Stimulating Literature Discussions.* Chicago: Blue Ribbon Press. Available from M. Kroll, 1717 Lakeview Drive, Darien, IL 60561.

Moffett, James, and Betty Jane Wagner. 1993. *Student-Centered Language Arts K–12.* 4th edition. Portsmouth, NH: Heinemann.

Nystrand, Martin, Adam Gamoran, and Mary Jo Heck. 1993. "Using Small Groups for Response to and Thinking about Literature." *English Journal* (January).

Oakes, Jeannie 1985. *Keeping Track: How Schools Structure Inequality.* New Haven: Yale University Press.

Ogle, Donna. 1987. "A Framework for Strategic Teaching." In *Strategic Teaching and Learning: Cognitive Instruction in the Content Areas.* Edited by Beau Fly Jones. Alexandria, VA: Association for Supervision and Curriculum Development.

Peterson, Ralph, and Eeds, Maryann. 1990. *Grand Conversations: Literature Groups in Action.* Ontario: Scholastic.

Postman, Neil. 1979. *Teaching as a Conserving Activity.* New York: Delacorte.

Postman, Neil, and Charles Weingartner. 1967. *Teaching as a Subversive Activity.* New York: Delacorte.

Probst, Robert. 1988. *Response and Analysis: Teaching Literature in the Junior and Senior High School.* Portsmouth, NH: Boynton-Cook.

Rief, Linda. 1991. *Seeking Diversity: Language Arts with Adolescents.* Portsmouth, NH: Heinemann.

Rogers, Carl. 1969. *Freedom to Learn.* Columbus, OH: Merrill.

Rosenblatt, Louise. 1938. *Literature as Exploration.* New York: D. Appleton-Century.

————1978. *The Reader, the Text, and the Poem: The Transactional Theory of the Literary Work.* Carbondale IL: Southern Illinois University Press.

Routman, Regie. 1991. *Invitations: Changing as Teachers and Learners K–12.* Portsmouth, NH: Heinemann.

Samway, Katherine Davies, Gail Whang, Carl Cade, Melindevic Gamil, Mary Ann Lubandina, and Kansone Phommachanh. 1991. "Reading the Skeleton, the Heart, and the Brain of a Book: Students' Perspectives on Literature Study Circles." *Reading Teacher* (November).

Schmuck, Richard, and Patricia Schmuck. 1988. *Group Processes in the Classroom.* Dubuque, IA: William C. Brown.

Short, Kathy. 1986. *Literacy as a Collaborative Experience.* Ph.D. Dissertation, Indiana University.

Short, Kathy Gnagey, and Kathryn Mitchell Pierce, eds. 1990. *Talking About Books: Creating Literate Communities.* Portsmouth, NH: Heinemann.

Slavin, Robert. 1985. *Learning to Cooperate, Cooperating to Learn.* New York: Plenum Press.

Smith, Karen. 1990. "Entertaining a Text: A Reciprocal Process." In *Talking About Books: Creating Literate Communities.* Edited by Kathy Short and Kathryn Mitchell Pierce. Portsmouth, NH: Heinemann.

Taylor, Denny and Catherine Dorsey-Gaines. 1988. *Growing Up Literate: Learning from Inner-City Families.* Portsmouth, NH: Heinemann.

Thayer, Louis. 1981. *Fifty Strategies for Experiential Learning.* San Diego, CA: University Associates.

Thelen, Herbert. 1954. *The Dynamics of Groups at Work.* Chicago: University of Chicago Press.

Vygotsky, Lev. 1978. *Mind in Society: The Development of Higher Psychological Processes.* Cambridge, MA: Harvard University Press.

Wheelock, Anne. 1992. *Crossing the Tracks.* New York: The New Press.

Wood, George. 1992. *Schools that Work.* New York: Dutton.

Zemelman, Steven, and Harvey Daniels. 1988. *A Community of Writers: Teaching Writing in the Junior and Senior High School.* Portsmouth, NH: Heinemann.

Zemelman, Steven, Harvey Daniels, and Arthur Hyde. 1993. *Best Practice: New Standards for Teaching and Learning in America's Schools.* Portsmouth, NH: Heinemann.